Praise for
*The Wall Street Professional's
Survival Guide*

"The author shares with the reader over 20 years of accumulated knowledge in dealing with job searches. A most timely book for those adversely affected by the vicious downsizing the labor force has experienced. Read it and improve your odds of regaining entry into the labor force!"
　　　　　　—Leon G. Cooperman, Chairman and CEO, Omega Advisors, Inc.

"Great brands endure through the ups and downs of business. Roy Cohen's career program will help you get the job you need in any market and power up your personal brand for long-term success. He's one of the smartest career coaches around."
　　　　　　　　　　　　—Barbara Corcoran, founder of The Corcoran Group

"Roy Cohen masterfully addresses all elements of a job search from self assessment to job negotiation strategies in his book *The Wall Street Professional's Survival Guide*. Cohen presents this information through logical steps and exercises, which enables the job seeker to use this book as a practical working guide. To illustrate the points, Cohen skillfully provides examples from his vast experiences as a professional coach. The valuable information in this book is relevant to the recent college graduate and to the experienced finance industry professional."
　　　　　　—Meg Flournoy, Associate Director, Student and Alumni Services,
　　　　　　　　　　The Fuqua Career Management Center, Duke University

"Every page in this book contains at least one invaluable nugget of wisdom to make your job search more effective. Use it as your guide for getting the attention you want and the job you deserve."
　　　　　　—Lois P. Frankel, Ph.D., author of the international bestsellers
　　　　　　　　Nice Girls Don't Get the Corner Office and *See Jane Lead*

"Frank and insightful, Roy Cohen provides a practical roadmap for any finance professional in transition."
　　　　　　—Maryellen Reilly Lamb, MBA Career Management, The Wharton School

"With great jobs on Wall Street difficult to find, Roy Cohen's career counsel is invaluable. This book brings to life the tools that job seekers need to prevail in a complex and dynamic marketplace."
　　　　　　—Richard J. McNulty, Tuck School of Business at Dartmouth,
　　　　　　Executive Director, Career Development Office and Executive Director,
　　　　　　　　　　　　　　　　　　　　　Center for Leadership

"In a job world turned upside down by the global financial crisis, Roy Cohen has produced a roadmap for those intrepid souls who wish to begin careers anew— whether in finance or elsewhere. It is never easy to start over, particularly if one is middle aged, but the rewards can be great, both financially and more importantly with relationships. Roy Cohen has written a work about life's lessons and renewal opportunities. It is a very good read."
　　　　　　—William W. Priest, Chief Executive Officer, Epoch Investment Partners, Inc.

"Whether you've just been laid off or are transitioning into the buy-side or sell-side, Roy Cohen's book will guide you through the process. Cohen helps Wall Street professionals navigate their way through a job search from self assessment and resumes to networking, interviewing, and negotiating. His exercises, sample responses to interview questions, and resume suggestions are great resources to job seekers. With almost 200,000 layoffs on Wall Street over the past two years, this is essential reading."

—**Matthew Temple**, Director of Alumni Career Services, Kellogg School of Management, Northwestern University

"It's great to be able to direct our students and alumni to this refreshingly frank book written by a respected industry insider. Roy provides the real deal on the job market, from assessments and referrals to transitions and separations, with interesting real-world examples to drive home his points. This is just the sort of practical and substantive information needed for those navigating a Wall Street career."

—**Regina Resnick**, Assistant Dean and Managing Director, Career Management Center, Columbia Business School

"Roy Cohen is America's top Wall Street career coach. This timely book will save and redirect many a career. Roy will show you how to do it, whether you are entry level or a top executive. No one in America has Roy Cohen's experience and insight in helping Wall Streeters with their careers. He knows the language and the solutions to their career-related problems."

—**Kate Wendleton**, President, The Five O'Clock Club

THE WALL STREET PROFESSIONAL'S SURVIVAL GUIDE

The Wall Street Professional's Survival Guide

Success Secrets of a Career Coach

Roy Cohen

Vice President, Publisher: Tim Moore
Associate Publisher and Director of Marketing: Amy Neidlinger
Executive Editor: Jeanne Glasser
Editorial Assistant: Myesha Graham
Operations Manager: Gina Kanouse
Senior Marketing Manager: Julie Phifer
Publicity Manager: Laura Czaja
Assistant Marketing Manager: Megan Colvin
Cover Designer: Alan Clements
Managing Editor: Kristy Hart
Project Editor: Jovana San Nicolas-Shirley
Copy Editor: Water Crest Publishing
Proofreader: Jennifer Gallant
Indexer: Lisa Stumpf
Senior Compositor: Gloria Schurick
Manufacturing Buyer: Dan Uhrig

© 2010 by Roy Cohen
Published by Pearson Education, Inc.
Publishing as FT Press
Upper Saddle River, New Jersey 07458

This book is sold with the understanding that neither the author nor the publisher is engaged in rendering legal, accounting, or other professional services or advice by publishing this book. Each individual situation is unique. Thus, if legal or financial advice or other expert assistance is required in a specific situation, the services of a competent professional should be sought to ensure that the situation has been evaluated carefully and appropriately. The author and the publisher disclaim any liability, loss, or risk resulting directly or indirectly, from the use or application of any of the contents of this book.

FT Press offers excellent discounts on this book when ordered in quantity for bulk purchases or special sales. For more information, please contact U.S. Corporate and Government Sales, 1-800-382-3419, corpsales@pearsontechgroup.com. For sales outside the U.S., please contact International Sales at international@pearson.com.

Company and product names mentioned herein are the trademarks or registered trademarks of their respective owners.

Printed in the United States of America

First Printing June 2010

ISBN-10: 0-13-705264-2
ISBN-13: 978-0-13-705264-6

Pearson Education LTD.
Pearson Education Australia PTY, Limited.
Pearson Education Singapore, Pte. Ltd.
Pearson Education North Asia, Ltd.
Pearson Education Canada, Ltd.
Pearson Educación de Mexico, S.A. de C.V.
Pearson Education—Japan
Pearson Education Malaysia, Pte. Ltd.

Library of Congress Cataloging-in-Publication Data

Cohen, Roy, 1955-
  The Wall Street professional's survival guide : success secrets of a career coach / Roy Cohen.
    p. cm.
  Includes bibliographical references.
  ISBN 978-0-13-705264-6 (hbk. : alk. paper) 1. Investment advisors. 2. Finance—Vocational guidance. 3. Job hunting. I. Title.
  HG4621.C622 2010
  332.6023—dc22
                            2009053246

To my clients to whom I'm deeply grateful:
Thank you for sharing your life's experience with me
and for trusting me to help you make the right career
decisions. I've learned far more than you can imagine.

Contents

Acknowledgments

This book would not have happened without the help of many individuals. Your support, guidance, and kindness have been undivided. Just thanking each of you seems somehow insufficient to express the depth of my gratitude. I hope you know how truly grateful I am for the gifts you have given me and in turn to the readers of this book.

First and foremost, I would like to thank Jeanne Glasser, Executive Editor at FT Press, for believing in a first-time author and for recognizing this book's unique message and the audience who would stand to benefit. I offer special thanks to my agent, Herb Schaffner, for introducing us and for taking me on as a client. You're a remarkable, patient fellow. And to Leah Spiro, formerly at McGraw-Hill, I thank you for taking a call from a complete stranger, for believing in the book, and for introducing me to Herb.

To the following friends and family: Arthur Dunnam, you heard me talk about this book forever. Now it's a reality. Thanks for encouraging me, believing in me, and promoting me. Next, Michael Fazio, whose own success served as the proverbial kick in the pants I needed to start this project. To Jeffrey and Darlene Rose, your friendship and wisdom mean the world to me. To Shirin Kerman and Monica Graham, thank you for your friendship and support. To Rob Pritchard for reading the draft…that's a loyal friend. To Maury Rogoff, my dear friend and PR magician, where do you get the energy? If only it could be harnessed. To Julie Bailey, you have been my mentor, advisor, and friend. To the members of the Nine o'clock Club, who for the past 14 years have inspired me and from whom I have learned countless lessons: Laure, Adrienne, Mary Lynn, Ellen, Brook, Carol, and Anna. To Sheryl Spanier, my friend, colleague, office mate, and cheerleader. To Kate Wendleton and the Five o'clock Club, the greatest job search and career management resource in the universe. What you've created is truly extraordinary. Thank you for allowing me to be a part of this amazing organization for the last 20 years. To my parents, who encouraged me to always go above and beyond.

Last but not least, I would like to thank the many clients I have had the good fortune to work with over the years. You have been the greatest teachers, and I have learned so much from you. I am grateful beyond words.

About the Author

Roy Cohen is a leading career counselor and executive coach. He is considered a subject matter expert and authority on Wall Street career management. For more than ten years, he provided outplacement services to Goldman Sachs, one of the world's foremost financial institutions. He is a popular speaker at a wide range of events and organizations, including: alumni groups from top business schools such as Wharton, Columbia, Chicago; New York Society of Security Analysts, Baltimore, Minneapolis, Stamford, and Philadelphia chapters of The CFA Institute; the Financial Executives Institute; Wall Street Rising; Rainbow/PUSH Wall Street Project Economic Summit; Urban Financial Services Coalition; Citibank Women's Leadership Council; and the Financial Women's Association. He is quoted often in the press (*Wall Street Journal*, *The New York Times*, *Business Week*, *Money Magazine*, and *Forbes* to name a few), and he has appeared on the Today Show and CNN. He has been associated with the Five o'clock Club since 1991 as a master coach, and he is a long-standing faculty member at New York University where he teaches in a program to train executive coaches. He holds an MBA from Columbia, a master's in counseling from Colgate, and an undergraduate degree from Cornell.

Visit his website at www.careercoachny.com.

1

The Wall Street Job Search:
Winning in Any Market

When new clients and prospective clients ask me how the process of job search unfolds, most of them want to find a job as quickly as possible, and they would like to know what steps I'll take to help them get there: when, where, and how? I've written this book because I've learned in coaching hundreds of clients that the vast majority of professionals are operating with passed-down wisdom, outdated advice, and popular magazine formulas for job search and career advancement that for the most part result in failure, particularly in a cyclical industry such as Wall Street. This book will not present formulas and 1-2-3 menus for succeeding at job search. However, there are secrets and rules of the road that are well known among leaders in my profession. They work.

Although each client and situation is unique, I've learned in working with thousands of clients for 20 years the quiet, powerful rules for taking control, secret shortcuts and time savers for getting your job target in focus, and money-wise techniques that cut through the bull and get you into the interview you need. In this book, I'll guide you through what I've learned over a lifetime of successful job search and career management in the financial services and banking industries. But first, here are the five attitudes you need to bring to this search and this book:

1. You must envision and believe you will succeed. This means more than being hopeful and optimistic; you have to believe that you deserve to win and will win.

2. You must accept that the process of job search is more complicated than it appears. Yes, you will respond to postings, contact recruiters, and sweat over your resume. But navigating your career is a process filled with contradictions, and is remarkably complicated in its execution. That's a second reason why I've written this book. If you learn the inside game of search, and follow the rules in this book, within a reasonable time frame and with reasonable expectations, you'll get a job...even in a horrible market. When the competition gets discouraged, you'll be there to clean up as they withdraw.

3. You must think long-term *and* short-term. The job you accept next may not rock your world, but it may get you closer to where you want to be. Don't eliminate options because they're not perfect or may even seem like a detour. In a tough market, virtually any option can be justified and used to position you attractively—and in good markets, the short-term position may be the perfect pivot to the great job you want.

4. You must persevere. Unlike most projects with a beginning, a middle step, and an end, there is no middle here. You start and you continue. It's over when you get an offer that you're willing to accept.

5. You must have a thick skin. Rejection in job search is inevitable. If you give in to your discouragement, you'll lose VALUABLE time and energy.

Before the search, take some time to understand the rules and secrets of job search—you're doing that by reading this book. Stage One is to define your target. Stage Two is to create a game plan or strategy that serves as a roadmap for your search. This includes all of the following and often much more:

- Your resume
- The pitch to position yourself and what you want
- The correspondence you write both to introduce yourself and to follow up
- Interview preparation and practice
- The companies you'd like to work for
- The various resources you'll use to get there, such as recruiters, job boards, social networking sites, and so on

The third and last stage is what I refer to as the "wagon"—but what I really mean is "falling off the wagon." It's very easy for smart people to get discouraged in job search. Face it; no one likes to get rejected, and that's what search is all about. You can't take it personally. When you fall off the wagon, you lose valuable time and you also make room for someone else to take the place that belongs to you. Don't let that happen.

Stage One of the Search: The List

The first stage of a job search is to define your occupational target or targets, writing them down in The List. The more targets you have on The List, the better. At this stage, you should rank the kinds of jobs you want in priority order, based on their desirability to you. These aren't companies, but positions. In this way, you won't feel like you're trying to be everywhere at once, crossing from one option to another, and you won't risk appearing unfocused to others. It is also more satisfying to be pursuing what you like best first without the distraction of options that have less attractive elements and the potential to produce feelings of disappointment. You'll be a lot more energized and committed to your search knowing that it's what you really want to do. If at some point, your first choice proves to be unattainable, then you know that you gave it your best shot.

We will give significant attention to the assessment process later on. Knowing we'll return to that, let's use an example to understand in detail how to create and work The List. Let's meet a former client, Eric, who was part of a downsizing at a large investment bank. He was a second-year VP in the technology investment banking group. Let's assume that Eric successfully completed a comprehensive assessment and generated the following targets:

- Investment Banks: The same position in an equivalent firm, a second-tier firm, or a boutique
- Corporate Positions:
  - Corporate Development (Internal M&A)
  - Strategy
  - Treasury
  - CFO, Director of Finance
  - Chief of Staff/Right hand to CEO/President
- Private Equity/Hedge Funds/Venture Capital
- Management Consulting
- Entrepreneurial: Buy or start a business, independent consulting, purchase a franchise
- Portfolio Management
- Sell-Side Research
- Ratings House
- Special Situations: Bankruptcy, turnaround management, restructuring

Eric considered each of these options and settled on finding a position in corporate development. As a backup, he would also pursue investment banking. The corporate development position would be his first choice, and he wouldn't turn to investment banking until he had exhausted the corporate path. At the time, opportunities in investment banking were readily available. There was no need to rush the process unless he was under pressure to land quickly. He wasn't. For Eric, quality of life assumed a prominent place as he prioritized his options. He had worked around the clock as a banker, and he was unwilling to make the same commitment going forward. He was also recently married and planning to start a family. Corporate development made great sense as an option. He could continue in a role that he enjoyed, and he could also exercise some control over his life and work schedule. He realized this wasn't a perfect solution, but the trade-offs were entirely reasonable: money for time.

Stage Two of the Search: The Plan of Action

The next stage after you've created The List is to develop your plan of action. These are the steps you'll take to move forward in job search. The Plan should include whom you'd like to speak to, where you'd like to work, what you want them to know about you, and how you would like the process to unfold. It's the resume, your pitch, the kinds of responses you give to interview questions, the correspondence you use to introduce yourself, and the follow-up you prepare after meetings. Think about this stage as a timeline and each of the items listed here as the tools you need to keep you moving.

That's exactly what Eric did. He used the following outline to organize his search:

- My target
- Why me, why this target: my qualifications, skills, and reasons to be taken seriously
- Specific or unique skills
- Examples of companies...a target universe

My Target: Eric determined that he would most like to work as a member of the corporate development team for a large company or as the head of this function for a small- to medium-sized company that could afford this function in-house. In both cases, it would have to be a company committed to growth through acquisition.

Why? Eric realized that he needed a defensible strategy to support his decision to shift the direction of his career. He would only feel comfortable presenting himself if he was absolutely and unconditionally convinced that this was the right decision for all of the right reasons. Although lifestyle was certainly a motivating theme, it was not one that would be appreciated by his audience as the primary reason for making a change. Imagine the reaction: We work hard here, too, or you make the big bucks so you should work hard. What were some of the more acceptable reasons to make a change?

- A desire to be a key member of an organization committed to its growth and success.
- Recognizing that churning one transaction after another without a direct and meaningful tie to a company was no longer satisfying.
- The need to have a more stable career.
- The potential to acquire equity over time rather than in sprints.
- Now that Eric was married, he and his wife were considering their options as a family. Hence, a commitment to re-locate to a family-friendlier community assumed a more important place on their list of priorities.

These were necessary but not sufficient reasons to explain the change. Yes, they provided context. Now it was up to Eric to demonstrate that his experience and qualifications would serve him well in this new role. Additionally, were there any distinctive skills that clearly distinguished Eric from other candidates? For example, did he offer an engineering undergraduate degree, a career in the military prior to his MBA degree, or some specialized knowledge?

Next, Eric generated a long list of target companies. These were companies that he would be willing and excited to work for if there were an appropriate opening. In fact, it didn't matter if an opportunity existed. That wasn't our goal. We just wanted to see what the universe of companies looked like. Was it large enough to support a search? Were the companies located in desirable communities?

He was ready now to create a resume. In truth, Eric already had one, but it wasn't customized around this new theme. He modified the resume, and then tested it among smart friends, colleagues, and a few former clients who worked in corporate development roles. He also practiced his pitch and story about changing the direction of his career. All feedback was duly noted, and if he found that the same comments continued to re-surface, it was factored into both the resume and the story.

Eric began to network and to respond to postings on job boards. With every conversation, he evaluated his presentation, and he paid particular attention to questions and topics that were more challenging for him. He also prepared boilerplate letters to streamline his speed in responding to ads. After networking meetings and interviews, he made sure to follow up with thoughtful, substantive correspondence. Staying on top of this stuff...the meetings, the referrals, the tips, the leads...involved a great deal of time and a huge amount of work. Nothing less than investing all of himself—every waking moment, every conversation—was acceptable to Eric.

Stage Three of the Search: The Wagon

How did Eric manage to keep himself from falling off the wagon? He couldn't. At various points during the search, he found himself completely and utterly depleted. It's only natural to lose steam even in the best-managed searches. Despite the fact that Eric was highly motivated, he was unprepared for the rejection that is inevitable in job search. He had always succeeded. In high school, college, and business school, he graduated at the top of his class. He won awards and scholarships. He was recognized and rewarded for being smart. So, for Eric, like many of us who do well academically, rejection implied failure.

He couldn't have been more wrong. To be successful in job search in a very competitive market, you have to expose yourself to rejection by relentlessly seeking interviews that can lead to your goal. This doesn't mean you should be indiscriminate by presenting yourself for opportunities that are clearly inappropriate. The more you do, the less control you have over who will make a decision about you and when that decision is likely to be made. Even more important to remember, in a tough market, no one wants to be responsible for adding headcount. It's a lot easier to get fired than it is to get hired. You may have made a dazzling impression, but the person making the hiring decision is accountable to his or her own superiors. He or she may not be comfortable taking a bold stand on a candidate, especially in an organization where cutbacks have happened.

All said, however, the more active you are, the more likely it is you will shorten the time it takes to successfully find the job you need and want. Obviously, this requires a sound strategy, but it also means redefining rejection. When you haven't heard back from a recruiter or your response to a posting goes unanswered, please don't presume it's because you don't measure up. You don't know why there is silence, and there is absolutely no benefit to speculating. Chances are, the position you are applying for has been put on hold or a recruiter has not heard back from his client company—you'll never know. If you are rejected, try to get information about who wasn't. Knowledge is power, and it also allows you to figure out how to make yourself an even stronger candidate.

What happened to Eric when he fell off the wagon? He stopped making phone calls and networking, he spent hours surfing the Web and playing computer games, he got a little cranky with his friends and family, and despite all of his free time, he was less likely to go to the gym, attend professional events, or network. He withdrew. How would he re-emerge? Eric would get back on the wagon when he received some sign from the market that he was still worthy...a call from a recruiter about an opportunity or a response from a resume he may have long forgotten was sent.

The irony is that much of this downtime could have been avoided. You must remind yourself daily (pray if you do, meditate, or write in a journal) that you and you alone are responsible for managing how much energy you devote. More activity always generates more interest. Inertia is reinforcing, and so is momentum. You just don't know when and in what form that interest will find its way into your inbox. *The lesson:* Take time to re-charge and to re-think your job search. Meet with friends and colleagues to get realistic feedback on what you're doing to promote your search and on how you can address challenges and roadblocks. Have some fun, too. A little play makes you a happier person, and that always comes across in your conversations.

The Process Simplified

I'm a big believer in shortcuts and visual devices to illustrate the process of job search. This exercise can easily be translated to a spreadsheet and, in fact, it should. For now, take a blank sheet of paper (8.5 by 11) and fold it in thirds.

At the top of the left fold, write the word "Options," and at the top of the right fold, write "Qualifications."

Options represent all the targets we have identified and could potentially pursue. As we will discuss in-depth in the chapter on assessment, they will be organized by priority and interest. Each of these sheets of paper gets only one option. Beneath that option, list all the skills, responsibilities, talents, and other prerequisites for successful candidates for this particular job. All of this information is readily available on job posting sites. If a job exists somewhere in the world, so does a great detailed description.

Beneath qualifications, match up yours line by line against the items listed in the left column. Where do you match up perfectly, and where are the gaps? For the matches, you will need to make sure this information is highlighted in your resume. For the gaps, are they real, and if so, how big are they? The decision then will be how to either address directly or minimize.

Next, in the middle section, write the word "Action Plan" at the top. Below it, list four roman numerals, as follows:

I. Target and Definition

This is the target you plan to pursue and its description.

II. Qualifications

These are the skills, experience, areas of expertise, and talents that you bring to this specific target.

III. Target List

This is the universe of companies where you can network and potentially present yourself as a candidate.

IV. Job Search

These are the mechanics of job search, getting out there and into the market. This includes the basics—how you actually conduct your job search: through ads and postings, networking, recruiters, and direct and targeted mail.

This is your starting point. It's where the rubber hits the road when you begin to job search. In later chapters, we'll cover various topics to support the execution of your strategy, such as resumes, your pitch, questions, and follow-up. For now, have fun folding paper.

2

You've Been Fired, Now What?

OK, it happened. The axe falls. No matter how much you've pre-pared for this moment or know that the market is to blame, you're still human. It's an emotional assault. It just doesn't feel right. Your boss and the HR person may have met with you. There are an infinite number of reasons to explain the separation: It's not working out, it's a numbers' game, you've been downsized or made redundant, there's been a RIF (also known as a reduction in force for the uninitiated), or your firm is cutting heads as a by-product of a takeover or merger. No matter what the reason, it's over. Now you have to move on. It won't be easy, it won't be quick to re-position yourself, and it certainly won't be pain free...which means you need to be on top of your game. On Wall Street and in financial services, significant down markets mean cutbacks, and for many industry professionals, the first bear market can be an ugly awakening to the fragility of their jobs.

You will feel that they screwed you. Whether it was your fault or not, the fact is you've been fired. Maybe it shouldn't have happened. Yes, you were working hard, and you may have even made money for the firm. Clearly, this was not enough when it comes to cutting bodies, especially in larger-scale reductions. Maybe they also shortchanged you on your severance package. That's what happens in a lousy mar-ket. Companies get cheap when they know they are disposing of staff. Some companies may be very experienced in terminating employees, and the process has been deliberately and systematically scrubbed to remove any potential landmines or potential for litigation. Other companies are surprisingly sloppy and uncomfortable in managing cuts, which may leave you with room to exploit their inexperience.

When it comes to cutting bodies, Wall Street firms don't generally care about the reasons why. Cutbacks can be triggered by a shrinking bonus pool or none at all, mergers, takeovers, bankruptcies, personalities, or politics. Whatever the reason, somebody is bound to get shortchanged. In this case, it was you.

Wall Street firms are also notoriously inefficient. You thought they were better managed? Historically, having a lot of money to burn meant that they had a lot of money to waste. So when the money disappears, the cuts are fast and furious. When downsizings happen in a tough market, there's a speed that prevents virtually any internal examination. The investment bank, hedge fund, or money manager isn't making money. That means the bonus pool will be diluted and that means people get fired. People get re-hired when profitability is restored. There is no institutional memory.

Despite occasional initiatives at some of the larger institutions to recognize and redeploy talent, it's not going to change. In fact, companies are making it easier to fire you. Some have established forced ranking systems where the bottom 25% is always vulnerable. The grading system is increasingly compressed so evaluations are less inflated and more likely deflated. If you find yourself in the bottom quadrant and your position has been eliminated, it makes an internal move a lot more challenging. It's probably impossible. If the scale is 1 to 5 (with 5 being outstanding and 1 or 2 representing a need for performance management), and you've moved from a 3 to a 2 or 1, I wouldn't recommend that you apply for a mortgage. You're probably out of luck and out of time.

So what do you do? The tendency among Wall Street professionals is to want to jump back in immediately. Taking action is good; acting impulsively is not. Please don't. I've seen far too many mistakes that could have easily been avoided if only patience and good judgment were exercised. Doesn't acting responsibly mean springing into action? Not when it comes to figuring out how to position the separation in the very best possible light. I know: Your urge is to solve the problem and restore the status quo, especially in a market where there are few opportunities. You want to get at them as quickly as possible. Please pay close attention. The path to career hell is paved with the very best of intentions. You need a game plan and an airtight alibi.

Preparing Your Separation Narrative

Why me? You can obsess over this question forever. The truth is, you will likely never know. Several reasons could have contributed, to a lesser or greater degree, to your separation, and if you examine your situation, they will be apparent to you. Your goal now is to decide which of these reasons will be least and most offensive and provide context as you tell your story. And that story is told honestly...in large part. All of the events are true. It's how you assemble them that requires a little extra creativity. There are an infinite number of approaches you can take to present the events. What can I state with complete confidence? I do know that some stories are better than others. I also know you'll lose valuable time re-examining the events again and again hoping to find some additional insight.

You work in a world where decisions are made quickly and transaction times are short. A sense of urgency is standard operating procedure. You cannot, and must not, reach for the phone before you've carefully thought through how you intend to position your separation and what you need to do to make it sound real. It's the game plan I mentioned in the preceding section. You've been dumped by your company. The best way to retain your market value is to make sure the story you tell presents you and these recent events in the right light.

John's Story

John is a senior institutional salesperson who was fired by a large investment bank. After junior sales stints at two other firms, he settled into a comfortable position where over time he was rewarded nicely and given coverage of larger and more important clients. He was completely and utterly blind sided when the separation occurred. He knew that cuts were about to be announced. He also believed, naively or not, that he was safe. He had a couple of good years, not great ones, but far better than several of his peers, and he also had good friends in senior management.

Like many of his colleagues on the trading floor, John is quick to take action. He's been socialized to expect immediate closure—typically short transaction times followed by clear measurable results. His initial reaction was to work the phones. He called just about everyone he knew in the business—clients, colleagues in his firm, and friends at other firms. Without thinking, he disclosed all the dirty laundry: what happened, when, and why. But all of this information was based on conjecture and an angry reaction to what he perceived to be a great injustice and an unfair situation. This was John's impression and not necessarily one shared by others...that is, until John's dramatic and unrehearsed telling of the tragic events.

In this heightened emotional state, clients like John do more damage than they realize. Full disclosure that is unfiltered wreaks real havoc. John was sharing the good, the bad, and the ugly regarding his separation, and he would discover that his audience was in large part unresponsive. No one wants or needs to know the absolute and complete truth. John was dumping the entire unedited version without anticipating how it would be received. Of course, everyone understood that he was upset, but they knew lots of other people who were fired, too. Why should John's experience be any different than theirs?

You cannot, and I emphasize, *must not* reach for the phone before you've carefully thought through how you want to position the separation. That's not so simple. There's a lot of information that needs to be sorted through and organized for its relevance in telling the story. You've been told by your company that you're no longer wanted. You're angry and frustrated, and maybe scared. Your mind is racing. This is the worst possible time to broadcast to your network any message. After all, you're not sharing a message; you're revealing dirty laundry, which is an unwelcome commodity in business. You want to share a narrative that is accurate, well-scrubbed, and calculated to tell your side of the story. Over-eager clients keep me in business. They tend to share the messy, unnecessary details. It's certainly not an unusual or unexpected response by individuals who are uncomfortable being removed involuntarily from the driver's seat, but it does make for a very bad impression, even among friends.

As difficult as it may be, lay low for a little while—please—at least until you're able to get your arms around what happened and have a story to tell that is convincing, simple, and not a burden for your audience to listen to. You need the time to sort through the details of the separation. What are the facts, what is fiction, and how much room is there for creative, yet truthful, interpretation? "Spin" control is critical. In the days immediately following the event, your brain is operating in overdrive. When your judgment is off, so is your story. Yes, getting fired feels like you failed, but it's often not about anything that you may have had control over: cutbacks, market downturns, politics, or shifts in strategy.

How to Explain the Separation

Sometimes the facts may not be enough. It's how they're presented that matters. For many people leaving jobs involuntarily, especially jobs that are high profile or highly compensated, there is a tendency to feel self-conscious and embarrassed about the separation. Your understanding of the issues and facts surrounding why you were separated from the firm is not always clear; your emotions are in overdrive during the weeks after you've left your employer, clouding cooler judgments. Over time, you'll need to work on a logical, but also a kinder and gentler, explanation that is reassuring to future employers. It may not seem so at first, but as the separation settles in, you'll get more comfortable with the story. That's why a time-out is so important. By taking a step back, you give yourself permission to examine the events rationally and your relationship to those events. I guarantee that the story gets easier to tell with some distance and perspective.

Initially, here's what John shared with the universe. It was not a pretty picture:

> The firm let us go. It's not the same place I joined 12 years ago. They really screwed us over. What a bunch of ungrateful, disorganized idiots. We were shortchanged on our bonuses, and the severance package really sucks.

Bitter doesn't work now. Companies don't want to hire employees with unresolved issues. It's far too complicated. In addition, talking about a disappointing divorce settlement—your lousy severance package, bonus, or some combination of the two—raises two concerns. First, it reflects that what really matters to you is what you'll get paid and not the work you'll be taking on. Second, it places you at a disadvantage when it comes to negotiating for your new position. If you let them know that you've been shortchanged and that you're also eager to return to work, you wave a big sign that reads: I am willing to be shortchanged again.

Here's how John re-told that story:

> As you probably know, there've been a lot of changes at _____. I made it through several waves of cuts, and I was finally caught up in this last round. It wasn't really a big surprise. My boss left the firm a few months ago, and a few of my colleagues left around the same time, too. I knew it was just a matter of time.

If pressed on how or why the separation happened, John could offer either of the following:

> The firm shifted the focus of the business away from (fill in the blanks here for whatever might describe your own situation). Of course, I'm disappointed, but as I mentioned, it wasn't a big surprise.

Alternatively:

> I'm restricted in what I can say about the separation. That's pretty standard for the firm. They've also been very generous in terms of severance, so I don't want to jeopardize that in any way. Let me just emphasize that I had a great career there.

If you don't have anything positive to say, then I suggest that you don't say anything at all. But please do try to give the impression that you and the firm parted amicably. You have absolutely nothing to gain by introducing anger or a desire for revenge. Save that for friends and therapists.

Ed's Story

Here's another example of re-constructing the details so that the story you tell is believable, truthful, and enhances you as a candidate. Again, the point is to scrub the information so that you remove or reposition key elements that may be difficult or awkward to share. If the separation has been documented and those files are readily available, you must exercise additional care with your narrative. In most cases, firms prefer to keep separation and related information unspoken, because documenting an employee's problem performance or behavior has the potential to expose them to costly litigation. That's also why your company most likely asked you to sign a waiver to get the enhanced severance package. It releases them from any further liability. It also means that you relinquish any right to sue, even if you feel like you have been mistreated.

Ed was working in a wholesaling role for a large investment management firm. He and his boss had a rocky relationship from the start.

His boss was a former career military officer and continued to see himself in that role in the private sector. Ed was a solid producer but a little bit of a maverick. He preferred to work independently and didn't like the idea of being micro-managed or, for that matter, being told how to get his job done. He was respectful, but it was clear to virtually everyone that he would do as he pleased...within reason, of course. To Ed, it was all about generating revenue. For his boss, it was much more about undivided loyalty and teamwork.

Ed and his boss co-existed in this non-confrontational stand-off for almost three years. Every so often, they would lock horns, but in large part, their issues were not officially acknowledged. It was an uneasy détente. The firm's headquarters were located in the Midwest. It was announced that Ed's regional office would be closed, and that this decision would also coincide with a large-scale reorganization. Ed's position was eliminated. He was offered the opportunity to re-locate to headquarters at a salary significantly below what he had been earning and in a position one level junior to his current level. It was clear that his boss wanted him out and was using the relocation to make that happen. He was also offered a severance package. Ed chose the latter.

Ed began to job search immediately. He had the good fortune of a large network to tap into and a reputation for being a good guy. Both have infinite value in terms of getting people to listen. What Ed didn't have was a good story. Here's how he was presenting the circumstances surrounding his separation:

> My boss and I have had a bad relationship from the very beginning. He and I just never got along...so when the relocation was announced, I knew there was no incentive for him to protect me. He could have if he wanted to...it was pretty clear to me that I needed to leave. They offered me the opportunity to move to headquarters, but at a price—a lower salary and a demotion.

No. No. No. Ed had all the right material to present the separation in a way that positioned both his divorce and his relationship with the company in a far better light. It was possible to be entirely truthful yet suggest a more amicable divorce. There was no need to focus attention on a bad relationship with his boss or the insult of being discounted. Together, we constructed an explanation that answered all the questions that could have been raised...or as many as he and I could think of. We anticipated potential landmines and addressed them preemptively.

Interviewers generally listen for inconsistencies and for incomplete explanations. Both will drive them to distraction, so it's up to you to keep them on target. Here's how Ed re-told his story. It's a response to the generic question: "What's going on?" Here's another way to ask that question: "When did you leave your company? Why?"

The following explanation is intended for Ed's network and for anyone else he's already acquainted with:

> Let me bring you up to date. There have been some very recent developments at _____. I'm in the process of winding down my position. It was in large part unexpected. Many of our activities have been relocated to _____ and I elected not to go. In truth, I thought that I was safe, but that wasn't the case.

If Ed is pressed further on passing on an opportunity in this market:

> My family, my professional life, my career, and my network are here. I'm not prepared right now to disrupt all of that.

For new contacts, Ed has no reason to tap dance. These folks didn't need to be "brought up to date." They just expected a quick, clear explanation:

> I'm in the process of winding down my position at _____. Many of our activities have been relocated to headquarters in a consolidation, and after a lot of soul searching, I elected not to go. My goal now is to _____.

Ed's example illustrates how you go about analyzing the events surrounding a separation. Like Ed, you select and organize those that need to be told and minimize those that should not. It is a simple story based on fact, but with a twist...sort of like the difference between a biography and a memoir: One is based entirely on fact, and the other on the creative presentation of that fact.

Getting Started After Separation

Right or wrong, you work in an industry where involuntary separation is often viewed as failure—the implication being that you're not tough enough or smart enough to succeed. You know intellectually that this is wrong, but it's hard to fight the emotional combat when you may partially believe there's some truth to the bias. That's the culture of many Wall Street firms and players, and the sooner you recognize the fact, the sooner you can put together your strategy.

You also need to acknowledge the reality that it will take time—potentially a good deal of time—to make an effective reentry. You'll be on the bench, so to speak, and this extended shelf life feels to many of us like a career death. You can cope with this anxiety by accepting and addressing the emotional fallout that is inevitable. It means acknowledging that job search may take a while, talking to others who've gone through similar journeys, and staying in touch with contacts and friends. If you jump prematurely into a new position before you've done your homework, it may turn out to be one more mess that will need to be neutralized and explained. The more of these you have, the more complicated the story. Here's how to get started after separation.

Step One: Attorney

Get the name of a great employment attorney and a recommendation for the best possible career counselor you can afford. This is not the time to think cheap. Inexperienced advisors may be less expensive, but you'll pay in the long run with information and resources that are untested and potentially damaging. Inexperienced advisors may also require many more billable hours to understand and process the situation. Therefore, a bargain by the hour may be cumulatively a very expensive mistake. There's no guarantee that any strategy you follow will be successful, so you want advisors who have been around the track and are deeply familiar with both your industry and the level at which you work. It might also be a good idea to establish a relationship with each of your advisors long before you need to take legal action or address important career matters.

Although it's unlikely you have a legal case, you really should check with an attorney to ensure that you're not agreeing to unreasonable conditions to receive your severance package. Most companies by now have been in the business of firing enough employees to have scrubbed the process for any potential landmines. I don't generally recommend that clients pursue litigation. Companies have pockets that are far deeper than yours...so even if you feel that an injustice has been committed, you may exhaust yourself financially in a legal process that could involve many, many years. That doesn't mean that you shouldn't engage in an aggressive and manipulative strategy to get a bigger settlement. All's fair in love, war, *and* involuntary separations.

Getting an attorney referral shouldn't be too complicated. Make a list of all the folks you know who've been fired in the last year or so. Realize that most separation agreements require a "gag" order. In accepting the severance package or one that's been negotiated, you agree not to disclose the terms of your separation. It's possible, then, that some of the people you contact may not be comfortable providing detailed information. If your contracts are concerned that your conversation may lead back to their former employer, reassure them that you don't want to know any of the details and that you would not do anything to jeopardize the terms of their separation. You just want an attorney referral...and only if the attorney was successful in negotiating the divorce.

Ask if they negotiated the separation using an attorney and, if so, were they satisfied with the legal representation. Would they recommend this attorney to negotiate aggressively, but not offensively, on your behalf? Will this attorney know with some certainty how likely you are to get some or all of what you want and on what items you need to compromise? Will he or she know whether or not you have a case and therefore grounds to pursue a fairer settlement?

Step Two: Counselor

When it comes to finding a career counselor, first ask friends and colleagues for referrals. Tell them you're at a turning point. Having the perspective of an unbiased and smart independent party can be invaluable during the highly stressful, emotional, and vulnerable time of job search and career development. A good career counselor or coach helps you think through your messages and approaches before you "go live" with the broadcast. As we've shown, getting on the phone immediately after the axe has fallen is a dangerous and ill-advised decision.

As an attorney advises you on negotiating your exit, a career counselor advises you on how to craft a story that supports your entry into a new organization, a story that positions you as attractively as possible. That's why it's a good idea to establish a relationship when you're at the top of your game and not when a crisis has hit. You want to work with someone whose judgment you respect and at a time of crisis—which is inevitable—will be there for you with sound shrewd advice.

Companies generally offer two levels of severance: the bare minimum, which is often an insulting number, and an enhanced package, if you agree to a variety of conditions. Most notable among those conditions...you forfeit your ability to sue the company at any point in the future. Severance is based on formulas, usually involving length of service and sometimes age. As a result of the WARN Act (Worker Adjustment and Re-Training Notification), companies with over 100 employees are required to provide notification 60 calendar days in advance of plant closings and mass layoffs. In lieu of the notification period, the two months is often paid in severance or alternatively, you remain as an employee of record and then transition to non-employee status after 60 days. In the latter case, stop working right this minute and begin your job search! Your company has fired you. You are no longer welcome there. You don't score any points by being a good employee, and you lose valuable time for job search.

Scripting What to Say When the News Is Delivered

You receive a call from your boss about a meeting. You show up, and the HR person is there, too. This is not a good sign. They explain to you that your position has been eliminated, they provide the details of the separation, and you are given a packet of information. Do not—I repeat, *do not*—sign any documents until you or an attorney or some other trusted advisor has reviewed the documents with you, and you understand your options. What are the terms of the severance? Will it be paid out in a lump sum or through payroll as if you were still an employee there? If the latter, what happens if the company goes bankrupt? Are there any conditions that prevent you from working in your industry and function for an extended period of time far beyond what is acceptable or customary for your industry?

There are lots of other questions that need to be addressed. For example, during the 60-day notification period, will you still have access to your phone and company email? How will the separation be presented to the outside world? That's why you need a day or two to digest the news and to understand what has been offered to you in your package. Chances are you won't have room to negotiate much, but it doesn't hurt to try. You have absolutely nothing to lose.

More important, what do you say or do in the separation meeting? Even if you were expecting to be fired, look and act stunned. This is not a joke. I'm serious. You are in a much better position to negotiate if you appear to be completely unprepared for this event.

If offered the opportunity to resign or be fired, suck it up and get fired. In a tough economy or market for your industry, it's easy to explain being separated as part of a downsizing. If you tell people you decided to leave on your own volition, either they'll think you're not telling the truth or that you're a fool. Why leave unemployment or severance benefits on the table? The exception: You're being fired for cause, and the company is letting you off the hook gently. It's your call, and it's a little more complicated when you have a U-5 paper trail riding on the decision.

Vanessa: The Separation Meeting and How to Explain

Vanessa worked for a global financial services organization in a client relationship management role. She was responsible for negotiating contracts for cash management services for key institutional clients and then coordinating the delivery of these services across the entire institution. It was a tough job with many moving parts and an unsympathetic, highly political boss—the kind of boss who had a reputation for throwing her people under the bus. Vanessa often found herself between opposing interests, and this was occasionally reflected in her performance reviews. They were decent but never stellar. Vanessa tried to please everyone but someone was always left expressing dissatisfaction...not necessarily with Vanessa, but with the process.

When Vanessa announced that she and her husband were about to adopt a baby overseas, she also explained that she would be leaving in two weeks to take FMLA (Family and Medical Leave Act). Although the bank provided up to three months' time off for adoptions, it felt as if she had committed a monumental act of treason. Her boss cut off virtually all communication. She was eliminated from distribution lists and not invited to important meetings. Both actions made it even more difficult for Vanessa to hand off her responsibilities and to provide a seamless transition.

About two months into the adoption, Vanessa received a message from her boss to schedule a phone meeting. It was with her boss and the HR person for her division. Vanessa was advised that her position was being eliminated. What the...! She got fired. Her boss got off the phone quickly and left Vanessa to discuss the details with an embarrassed and overworked HR person. She learned subsequently that a large number of other employees had been terminated, too. Still, it felt like she had been singled out.

Vanessa was angry and stunned. She was also fearful. Coincidently, her husband had lost his job just two months prior. What would happen to her, and how would she support her family? So many questions were racing through her head. It was certainly a theme that she and I had discussed over time, but when faced with the harsh reality of being fired, it felt final and terrifying. Here's how she handled the conversation with the HR person:

> I'm just devastated by this news. I can't believe that I'm being fired while on leave. You know, I just adopted a baby from overseas and my husband lost his job last month. Is this standard operating procedure for the bank? This is awful.

The HR person wanted to review the separation package on the call, but I had advised Vanessa not to have that discussion until she was thoroughly prepared and absolutely clear on what she wanted:

> I'm just so upset right now. I really can't focus on what you're saying. Is it possible for us to schedule a time to meet either by phone or in person? I'd prefer in person...with the baby at home, it's a little noisy.

The HR person agreed to a meeting. She discussed the terms of the separation, including its timing, severance, and medical benefits. Vanessa had two major concerns: when severance would begin and how her separation would be presented to the world outside. It became immediately clear that her return from FMLA had not been taken into account in determining the correct and official end date. Vanessa had also been planning to take a shorter leave so as to return to work as quickly as possible. Now that she was being terminated, why bother:

> Of course, you can understand that the adoption has been so much more involved than I initially imagined. I intend to take

my full three-month leave. My expectation then is that I'll also be eligible for the standard notification period before my severance kicks in. Yes?

That's what Vanessa got. She was also told that her separation was being treated as a downsizing. Good news! It's always easier to explain a separation that involves lots of people than a "one-off." Now to tell her story:

> I've made it through numerous cuts at the bank. I knew at some point, I might be vulnerable. We've had several major changes in top management in the division, and the focus of the business seems to be shifting. I've also been in my position for several years, and I'd recently begun to express an interest in transitioning into a new role...I just didn't expect to be cut while I was on leave to adopt my son.

We intended to induce sympathy for her as well as probable cause. How could they do something so nasty at a time that should be joyful? Yes, we implied, that's what big institutions do if they suspect you may be gearing up for a change in your personal life that will alter your relationship with the firm.

One Last Point: The HR Person

It's always a good idea to establish a friendly relationship with your HR person. I don't care what your personal views may be about the HR department and the people who work there. Lose them. You don't have to like the folks in HR or, for that matter, anyone in the organization. You just have to pretend to. It's about survival. It's also about managing your reputation, getting to know the right people, and above and beyond all else, making sure that you are in the loop regarding key events. If only Vanessa had worked this angle.

When it comes to negotiating your divorce from the organization, a good relationship with one or two well-placed HR managers will be invaluable. People take care of people they like and with whom they have a shared history. Your friends in HR generally know in advance about staffing changes, compensation, bonus numbers, colleagues who are in favor, and those who aren't.

I'm not suggesting that you go overboard to develop these relationships. It has to look and feel genuine. I'm referring to small gestures...expressions of interest and commonality that will unite you against the enemy: the organization you both work for. They'll come in handy when you most need them—when your goal is to strengthen and promote your reputation and career internally, and when you need inside information to maximize your take-out and a safe landing in a separation.

3

Self Assessment: The Secret Weapon of Job Search

Skilled professionals will "do their homework" to research a customer, a stock, an investing strategy, an important presentation, or any major decision at work. But many of us resist the opportunity of self assessment to better understand our own strengths, challenges, needs, and aptitudes for something as monumental as our career. I've never worked with a client who enjoyed the assessment process or the work involved. For many of them, assessment didn't come easily. What they liked, however, was the outcome. You may not enjoy the process either, but I encourage you to undertake it. I've logged the results over twenty years as individuals better understand themselves and their career direction, decide upon techniques and strategies to use in achieving their goals, and eliminate wasted time and frustration in pursuing wrong turns and options that don't fit their strengths.

Assessment takes time and patience. The results, however, can change the course of your life dramatically and position you for growth and opportunity. Be warned, though: The process is tedious, one-sided, and lonely. There's no reliable way to measure your progress other than the "a-ha" moment when insights occur and release their powerful energy and sense of purpose as you see the way forward. There are no real shortcuts to improve the quality and depth of the personal data you collect.

The exercises provided in this chapter will help you understand and define your options. As you go through the process, you will learn the language of self-discovery. Stick with the process, and you will discover a clearer sense of purpose, a new ability to see the path ahead, and the steps required to take it. The exercises will reveal the activities you enjoy, your skills, aptitude, core values, *and* your dislikes, areas of weakness, and low-priority values. A great deal of behavioral and cognitive research agrees that building on individual strengths and skills is the proven path from good to great. Assessment sets you on this course.

After you complete the self assessment, I will guide you through the process of translating these insights into clear, realistic targets. These will be targets you can achieve within a reasonable period of time and, in large part, with the resources at your disposal. Sounds simple, right? It's not. Whether you've been working in the same career for a very long time or you're just starting out, translating the assessment results into a plan of action for your life is not easy. This is the "figuring out" part, and it often trips us up. It's pretty easy to make the lists that describe us. It's another far more challenging exercise to make some sense of the information you've gathered.

Why Bother?

Do you need assessment? Not necessarily. If you like what you do and opportunities still exist, don't waste your time. Go to the beach. See a movie. If you have no doubt about the next step in your career, you're eager to get the job search started, or if you can't, or don't want to, envision doing anything other than what you've always done, skip this chapter. There's no point...except to re-confirm what you already know: You like your job and your career, and you intend to continue working in this role. In that case, assessment is helpful as a reminder and as a tool for interview practice when you're asked about strengths, weaknesses, successes, and failures. It's also reassuring to know that you're on the right track. However, keep in mind that the global workforce of 2010 and beyond offers few safe harbors for professional job security, and this is particularly true in financial services. You may love your job, you may have a loyal supervisor and employer, but our global economy can produce shockwaves on any given instant that disrupt business conditions and assumptions. If you are reading this book because you absolutely, positively must find a job in the short-term, then skip this chapter, and return to it after you've found that short-term situation that meets your immediate financial needs.

If you like your career, but the demand for your occupation and skill set have evaporated or diminished, assessment will help you understand how to use your skills in related industries. For example, if you've worked on the trading floor, you might consider looking at financial information companies such as Bloomberg or Thomson Reuters, vendors who provide support to the world you know well. Assessment will help you identify key skills and qualifications that are transferable and relevant. You will protect your compensation level and leverage your experience more effectively if you move into functions and roles that require the skills and credentials you've developed.

Here's another common situation. What if you like what you do, and you know opportunities are abundant, but you've been repeatedly passed over for promotion? Assessment can generate insights into what's not working for you and guide you in identifying techniques and suggestions to make you more competitive in your current career track. It may also point out new options and directions where success will be more likely to be achieved.

Another scenario: You've either lost your job or you're feeling vulnerable or maybe you just hate what you do. What you do is no longer valued. There are many, many more qualified candidates than positions, if any. Got the picture? The market sucks. If you don't have a clue about options or direction, you need assessment...right now.

A lot of you reading this book probably fall into this category. The period between 2008 and 2010 ended entire companies and hundreds of career options. The need to radically revise our career possibilities and plans is often forced upon us by market forces. What you do...whether you loved or hated it...may no longer exist or doesn't exist right now. You've got no choice but to figure out what's next, and that means taking the time to explore new options.

Is this process a waste of your time? How long will it take? Could you buy this information off the Internet? No! Is there someone who can untangle the cobwebs and tell me precisely, quickly, and clearly what I should be doing with the rest of my life? Is that what career counselors do? No! They can't, and shouldn't, do the work for you. They can, however, point you in the right direction and help you to avoid unnecessary detours and distractions. A good career counselor will keep you focused and prevent you from getting discouraged.

That being said, you shouldn't expect the assessment process to be open-ended. Unless you're independently wealthy (which I expect eliminates virtually everyone reading this book), you can't afford a long process. More important, you need to translate research into action because the excitement of discovery, of getting results, and the rush that happens when you have a breakthrough, will keep you motivated and reinforce your efforts.

Another secret: The more assessment you do, the faster you'll figure things out. It's your life and your career. Important, I assume. When a company plans for the future, it usually engages in a detailed, comprehensive planning process. Why? No doubt, to remain profitable both now and in the future and to determine strategies to get there. Why should you deserve any less attention and commitment?

Let's Get Started

What follows are a series of exercises and examples. Do all, some, or none. Take the time to really think about what you're being asked. It's about quality and thoughtful examination over volume. Don't rush to finish the individual exercises. You might even try some of them more than once to see if there's consistency and commitment in your thinking. Alternatively, it's interesting to see if new ideas or perspectives emerge.

Remember that assessment is not an answer; it's a tool. The more you think about who you are and what you want (and don't want), the more likely you'll figure out a next step and a step beyond that. No single exercise is intended to produce immediate insight...so if you're looking for an immediate answer, you're going to be frustrated, angry, or disappointed. Please don't blame your career counselor either, unless, of course, he or she deserves it.

This isn't an exam or test with right or wrong answers. Assessment is about asking questions and paying close attention to your answers. Assessment requires thinking about those answers. It requires keeping track of information and organizing it so that key themes and ideas emerge about career direction and options.

We'll examine a few approaches that have been successful for a good number of clients I've worked with over the years and during other meltdowns in the markets. You'll benefit from economies of scale. Of course, client names and some of the details have been modified to protect the innocent and to make for better reading! Learning through illustration has always been more effective for me personally, so I'll assume the same for you. Some points to bear in mind as you proceed:

1. An open mind is vital. You don't know what will work for you, so please don't pre-judge.

2. Involve others in this process. Opinions of people who know you well are useful.

3. Don't try to rush through the exercises. Take your time, set them aside when you're distracted, and don't force it when you're tired.

4. Re-visit and re-read the exercises after they're completed. New insights are possible and always welcome.

5. Don't lose this stuff.

Exercise 1: Describe an Ideal Day

If you could spend a day doing anything and everything you'd like, what would you be doing? Where would you be? Who would you be with? Yes, it's a fantasy, but it doesn't have to be outrageous. It could even involve work. It's whatever you would enjoy and however you choose to spend your time. It begins from the moment you wake up until the time you go to sleep. What are you wearing? How about your meals? Be as explicit as you'd like. It's your fantasy, your life, and your adventure. Write a paragraph or several pages. Just make sure it's thorough.

This exercise is intended to get you to think about how you spend your time and when you feel the greatest satisfaction and joy. Wouldn't it be terrific if these themes could be identified and then transferred to the kind of work you do?

So, once you've finished the exercise, either review it on your own or ask a person whose judgment you trust to offer you feedback. What are the takeaways? What is noticeably absent?

A while back, I was working with a client, Rob, who lost his job in institutional sales. He'd been unemployed for six months by the time we were introduced. Initially, he took the summer off to travel and to spend time with his family. He planned to start his search after Labor Day. I'm a big believer in corporate delinquency and often encourage clients to take as much time off as they want to and can afford to. Just know that when you return to job search, it will still be there...as huge and unwelcome as you expected it to be. I've often found that clients go into a time off period clear and comfortable with the decision. But when the time comes to return, they become even more nervous despite it being a conscious decision.

For Rob, the challenge he faced, in addition to returning from his summer sabbatical, was an increasing lack of interest in trading. He felt that he had outgrown the role. The excitement was no longer there. It had disappeared a few years ago, and what remained was just a familiar routine with little satisfaction.

Rob was 38 at the time, and he and his wife had two kids in their early to mid teens. The family lived modestly considering his career and relative success. He'd been very conservative about spending and had accumulated substantial assets. His wife was ready and wanting to return to work, too, and this offered an additional dimension to consider in exploring options and expectations for compensation.

I asked Rob about his background. He came from a large working class family and was raised in a suburban community north of New York City. Education was an undebatable priority for all of the kids. No exceptions.

Rob, his wife, and children now lived in New Jersey, and he'd been commuting to lower Manhattan for ten plus years. As a parent, Rob was active in coaching soccer and little league in his community. I asked him about other interests and organizations. He explained that one of his siblings passed away at an early age from a serious illness, and that he, Rob, was now very active in fundraising initiatives to help find a cure for this disease. He spoke about his involvement with both passion and a sense of purpose.

Rob completed several of these exercises, and because it was by far the exercise he had written the most about, we paid particular attention to his "Ideal Day." In it, Rob described in great detail and enthusiasm what his day would look like as if he'd been thinking about this for years and storing it away for the right moment to disclose. Among the many activities that he envisioned was a hugely successful fundraiser for his brother's charity.

A-ha! We were on to something. That's how self assessment works. You find a thread, you work with it, and hopefully it leads you in the right direction. In this case, Rob decided to explore careers in fundraising and development for the not-for-profit world...hospitals, schools, medical research, and educational organizations. The list was virtually endless, so we took a second thread and wove it into the equation: education, an ongoing and lifelong theme for him. Rob is now working as a development director for a business school that's part of a major university. Although the salary was initially a shock, especially since he first joined in a junior role, he loves the work, the lifestyle, and the role he plays in helping to support an important educational mission. How he made the move is the subject of another chapter.

Exercise 2: Likes and Dislikes

In this exercise, describe every job you've ever had in a sentence or two; then list what you liked about the job and what you disliked. Memory is critical to the success of this exercise. We tend to smooth out the edges with a pastel hue. Over time, even horrible situations don't feel as intensely unpleasant. It's a common reaction, of course, but unfortunately one that allows us to repeat bad experiences. Also, your reactions at the time may be far different from how you would react today. You've grown up—it takes a lot more than having a trader throw a phone at you to get you angry...or at least, you know how to avoid flying objects.

How you feel today is not the point here. Your goal is to recall what you liked or disliked about the job at that very point in time. Please don't edit as you go. Write down your memories, your reactions to those memories, and your feelings.

Why is this exercise useful? Having worked with thousands of clients, I can tell you without any reservation that those who like their jobs are happier. Obvious, right?

> Gina was a sixth-year associate in the securities practice at a large well-regarded law firm. She was a magna cum laude graduate of a top undergraduate school and before she became a lawyer worked full-time as a paralegal in the legal department of a global consumer products company while attending law school at night.
>
> Gina and I met shortly after she was passed over for promotion to partner. The firm advised her that she would be terminated, not because of any deficit in her legal skills, but due to her

attitude and commitment. She had been questioning a law firm career for several years by now, and it apparently surfaced in her interactions with colleagues and clients. Gina was well-liked by almost everyone. She was just viewed as not being committed to her career. In fact, when her colleagues were surveyed as to their willingness to serve as references, most expressed very conflicted feelings about her separation: a great friend, a smart lawyer, but always dissatisfied with her responsibilities, and a little sad, too. Gina could not disagree.

In completing this exercise, Gina explained that she, at age 33, had only worked in two real jobs in her entire career. In high school and college, she had lots of summer and work study positions but those were by now a blur. She felt as if she had been short-changed; I, on the other hand, was delighted. For the purposes of this exercise, it's easier and faster to dig deeper with fewer moves. In addition to listing her likes and dislikes as an attorney and paralegal, I asked her to broadly describe how she felt about all of those assorted part-time and temporary situations: medical billing at a doctor's office, assisting a professor in his research, nanny, and waitress. I instructed her to write about her overall impressions of the jobs, not the details.

The exercise resulted in some interesting and not terribly surprising feedback: Gina loved being a lawyer, but she hated working for a law firm. She enjoyed being viewed as a subject matter expert on the securities industry and she liked being part of a team. What she hated, yes hated, was the unpredictability of her schedule. It became clear very early on in our discussions that Gina favored situations that provided structure and control. She was also at a point in her life where she wanted to focus attention on life outside of work...translation: to get married and have a family.

From her notes regarding the hodgepodge of jobs before and during college, it was also clear that Gina preferred to work independently without layers of decision making and reporting. She wanted to be the point person, the place where the buck stopped. She liked to be the boss...Nanny Gina! She was also the waitress who never screwed up an order.

It occurred to both of us that Gina's likes and dislikes led us both down the same path: a love for the law, deep knowledge of the securities industry, subject matter expert, independent yet indispensable member of the team, and a need to establish clear boundaries around work. She eventually joined an investment bank in its capital markets division as an in-house attorney.

Alternatively, the "Likes and Dislikes" exercise can be expanded into what I refer to as the Kitchen Sink exercise. It's just bigger. How does it work? It's very simple. Just answer the following questions:

1. What do I like to do? At work and outside of work?

2. What don't I like to do? At work and outside of work?

3. What's important to me? In life, at work?

4. What are my strengths?

5. What are my weaknesses?

6. What am I recognized for being good at?

7. What do people think I'm weak at?

8. What comes naturally to me?

9. What do I have to work hard at?

10. What kinds of people do I prefer to be around?

Exercise 3: Who Do You Most Admire and Why?

We can learn a lot about ourselves by looking at who we most respect and admire. Why did you select these people? What is it about them that makes them different, better, and stand apart? Are there characteristics and traits that inspire us and that, given the right opportunity, we would strive to embrace and emulate? It doesn't matter who these people are: family members, friends, business colleagues and business heads, historical or political figures, religious leaders, celebrities, or athletes. They can be living or deceased. Imagine if you were successful in finding a job that allowed you to fully express these characteristics.

The opposite of this exercise offers equally interesting insight. Who do you most dislike, assuming there is such a person for whom you have extreme and very negative feelings? Rather than focusing on characteristics to mirror, view them as qualities in a boss that make for a bad marriage.

> Claire was until recently a senior credit risk manager for a large institutional asset management firm. She's in her late 40's and has worked in credit for her entire career. She's considered an expert in credit derivatives and other complex structured products and in assessing hedging techniques.
>
> Claire joined a ratings house right out of college and found herself, and for no particular reason, in a newly established structured products ratings group. While there, she sat for and passed all three levels of the CFA exam and was awarded the designation. After a couple of years, she was recruited by a major investment bank, and then a few years later following a re-organization, she joined another firm. Eventually she was offered the opportunity to move to the buy-side, and for various reasons, primarily related to lifestyle, she made the move.
>
> Claire is a single, devoted parent with a special needs child. Her teenage daughter was enrolled in a private school, and Claire maintained an active relationship with her daughter's teachers and other faculty and staff. She loves the school and has seen her daughter make great progress there.
>
> When we met, Claire shared with me her feelings of boredom with her work and a desire to make a change in her life. She was also willing and financially prepared to take time off—in fact, as much time as she needed—to make this happen. She was ready.
>
> It took Claire only a few minutes to complete the "Admire" exercise. It was obvious to her who she most respected and admired—one of her daughter's instructors. Claire believed that this fellow was responsible for a major breakthrough. What did she admire most about him? He was compassionate, smart, passionate about his work, and according to Claire, he was making a real difference in the world. Pretty powerful!

Fast forward, Claire applied to an accelerated master's program in education with a specialization in working with special needs students. She's in school now and, according to a recent email she sent me, loving every moment. Yes, the money will be far below what she earned even at the very beginning of her career, but that's no longer a priority for Claire.

Exercise 4: Who Do You Most Envy and Why?

Envy may be one of the seven deadly sins, but when it comes to insight with respect to careers and job search, envy generates a wellspring of valuable information. What is envy? For the purposes of this assessment exercise, it's thinking that someone has something you want—an advantage—and feel that you deserve.

Of course, some of what we envy may be unachievable under any circumstances, no matter how favorable: to be born rich, to resemble Brad or Angelina, or to be recognized as a great and brilliant thinker. On the other hand, much of what we envy may be just a byproduct of hard work, ambition, good fortune, and timing. We eliminate those individuals whose assets are innate.

Identify a few people...say five...who you envy. Just like the "Admire" exercise, they can be virtually every or anyone. Then, in a paragraph for each, explain why you chose these five and what it is about them that you would like to have as your own.

When I first met Dave, he was on his way out of a large investment bank, exiting involuntarily. He began his career there following business school and joined the firm as an associate in corporate finance. I would describe Dave as an Ivy League scholar-athlete with an edge. He was unexpectedly modest and expressed surprising self-doubt about his capacity to be successful. Imagine a cross between Clark Kent and Woody Allen.

After two years, he felt like he was on the wrong track and had the opportunity to transfer to the wealth management division as an institutional client relationship manager. This also turned out to be a poor fit. Although the new post was interesting at first, it wasn't long before Dave, despite his best intentions, began to disengage and go through his routine without much passion. He discussed his dissatisfaction with his boss—generally not a good idea unless your goal is to be "packaged out"—and when the next round of cuts happened, he was at the top of the list. Remember, he had moved internally just two years before.

Dave complained to me that he was lagging behind his more successful classmates from B-school. It seemed at the time that money was a motivator for Dave as well as his own measure of success. I asked who he most envied, and he listed several of his friends who were working in institutional sales. If money was his primary motivator, then it was clear that we had a target to pursue.

Dave joined another global investment bank and had considerable success in sales. Again, he found himself after two years in much the same place as before: bored with work, and seeing no potential for growth and change. So, it wasn't entirely the money, he discovered. Dave needed to be intellectually challenged. What he had also proven over those two years was that he could compete and win. He was back on track, although not entirely satisfied.

What next? I asked Dave the same question as before. Who did he most envy? He explained that his work involved frequent conversations and meetings with portfolio managers at hedge funds and asset management firms. He enjoyed the conversations, particularly those that were more challenging and even at times confrontational. He knew that it was important to demonstrate value and logic, and he appreciated the concerns expressed by the portfolio managers. He envied them for the role they played in evaluating and managing investment options, and he also knew firsthand their potential to be well compensated. We were headed in the right direction. Dave eventually joined a large fund of funds manager as an analyst.

Exercise 5: Write Your Biography

Whenever I'm contacted by a new client, I always request that he or she prepare a biography in advance of our first meeting. It's an information gatherer for me, shorthand so to speak, which allows me to get to know a client before we actually sit down face to face. If you think about it, it is also a money saver. This means I don't need to review this information in a meeting, and can therefore start the process sooner. Why waste time and discuss what I already know? Of course, when the need to meet is urgent or a crisis may be imminent, such as a termination or a bad review or an unexpected offer, then we break the rules...but generally not.

Nowadays, the biography exercise helps me separate the grown-ups from the dabblers and whiners:

Gee, that sounds like a lot of work....

No one has ever figured me out, so why invest a lot of time and effort when the process hasn't moved far enough along....

I'd rather just tell you in person.

I recommend the biography exercise for those of you working on your own with this book, or with a career counselor as well. The biography is essentially a detailed history and provides as much or as little information that you're comfortable sharing: where you grew up, what your folks did or do, siblings, where you went to college and why, summers and how spent, life after college, the various jobs you've held, and what you did in them. It should include the high and low points; the good, the bad, and the ugly. It should detail experiences that may have been unpleasant, bosses who tortured you, and decisions that you made which at the time may have seemed right, but now in hindsight were anything but.

Why the bio? Collectively, our experiences offer some understanding and insight about how we make decisions, what motivates us, our successes and failures, where we feel that we have achieved our potential or will, and where we may feel that we have failed. It will draw out key themes that have defined your career up till now.

> Andrew and I met several years ago. He's a hyper, high-energy fellow, very bright, outgoing, and generous to a fault. He's well-liked but not particularly good at managing political relationships. Like Gina, Andrew is trained as an attorney and was a senior associate at the time of our introduction. Like Gina, he too attended a top undergraduate school. He then proceeded immediately on to a good law school, where he excelled and graduated at the top of his class. Throughout his three years there, Andrew repeatedly questioned his decision to pursue a legal career. It never felt right. He found himself often contemplating dropping out and applying to MBA programs, but ultimately he decided to stick it out.
>
> Andrew's grandfather established a successful apparel manufacturing company, which his father later ran. From an early age, Andrew was actively involved in virtually every aspect of the business. Did he like the apparel industry? Not really. It was comfortable and familiar, the decision-making process came naturally to him, and he could also get his arms around the end-product and its ultimate value. He didn't have the same connection to the law.
>
> After graduation, Andrew joined a mid-sized law firm in its real estate practice. His family owned a significant amount of commercial property, and he had always taken an interest in its management. At the time, he saw this as a way to bridge his interests and skills. The problem was, he had no passion for the law in any context.
>
> What did Andrew's bio tell us? A few key themes emerged. First, he preferred to be the driving force behind a transaction. This often led to confrontation and conflict at his firm and with clients...he believed that he knew better or was smarter than many of them, and he had great difficulty suppressing his opinions. For Andrew, it was speak out or get an ulcer.
>
> Although Andrew appreciated the knowledge he had acquired over the years as a real estate attorney, he often felt frustrated serving in a secondary role. He wanted to be the person to identify the deal, to hire outside counsel to hash out

the complex legal matters, and to take both the credit and bear the responsibility for the success or failure of the transaction. He also liked business, and that's the standard by which he wanted to be measured: through clear, objective metrics, not on legal or intellectual prowess.

What happened? Andrew joined a real estate investment fund, initially working in a quasi-legal, quasi-business role. It was a cross-over role. He could contribute immediately as an attorney and also come up to speed as an investment manager. The goal: to eventually move to the business side. He was thrilled. How did he find the position? Remember, Andrew is naturally outgoing. He has a large network of friends who were available and willing to support his decision once he was absolutely clear on what he wanted to do. It was just a matter of time and telling the right story.

Exercise 6: The Lottery

Yes, this is the fantasy exercise. What would you do with a windfall or its equivalent? This is a career counselor's assessment staple, included in one form or another in many career books. If you didn't have to work for money, what kind of work would you do? Yes, you still have to work. That's the point of this exercise. No glib easy responses. If you want to be at the beach, then it's either the concession stand or the lifeguard station. Better start pumping up now.

If you're having trouble coming up with an actual job or role, then just describe *aspects* of the kind of job in which you'd thrive. What skills would you use? What kinds of people would be your associates? How would you be dressed? Where would you live and work? What special experience or qualifications would you bring to the role? In addition, describe what you would not want in a job. What would make a job absolutely, unconditionally unappealing? One technique is to envision the "worst possible job" for you and your talents. Don't hold back; include it all.

Maria was born in Cuba and raised in Miami, the daughter of hard-working and very ambitious parents. From an early age, she felt destined for a career that would involve international travel and overseas experience. Not sure what that would be or how to even define, she was determined to attend college away from her home in Miami. That decision led her to New York and a scholarship to Columbia University. She was also successful in obtaining summer positions at various financial institutions. Upon graduation, she was hired for an entry level position in international private banking. Maria viewed this as a stepping stone, and in two years, she applied to a joint MBA/international affairs program at Wharton and the Lauder Institute.

It was an exciting time for Maria. By now, she spoke Spanish and English as well as Portuguese, and she was recruited for a number of emerging markets positions focused on Latin America. It seemed like all of her dreams were becoming a reality. She joined a top investment bank in research. She was promoted within three years to VP and seemed to be on a fast track. Then the bottom fell out. The market crashed for Latin America, and Maria lost her job. She was devastated; she had never failed before, and that's how she perceived the separation.

Maria was recruited almost immediately by another bank, a second-tier institution. The situation felt like a serious step back and an even bigger letdown: the money, the prestige, and her role were all diminished. In completing this exercise, Maria wrote about her parents and their struggles to start a new life in the United States, the community in which she was raised, and her growing feelings of emptiness in her work. It was a sad story for a woman with so much promise and talent.

If money were not an issue, what would she do? She liked finance and banking and she enjoyed having global responsibilities, but she also wanted to feel like she was doing something to make the world a better place. Several options emerged: the World Bank, the IMF, micro finance, and project management in global philanthropy, to name a few. Money was, in fact, an important item on Maria's checklist that we could not ignore. She is now an officer for an international financial institution that provides support to developing countries.

Exercise 7: My Jobs

Saving the best for last, here is a simple exercise: List all of the jobs you've ever had, or as before, those that you can recall with sufficient clarity and detail. If you've had ten jobs in one company or you've worked for ten companies in different roles, list all ten and describe each to the best of your ability and memory. You don't need to provide exact dates—just a sentence that explains the essential reason for the job; for example: emerging markets research analyst Latin America, senior compliance officer for a fixed income trading division, or M&A banker specializing in hi-tech clients.

Under each job, make a list of accomplishments that you feel were directly due to your being in that role. The accomplishment may or may not have been acknowledged by the firm. It doesn't matter. It's all about what you think, not them.

Next, under each job, list any disappointments, regrets, or embarrassing events that may have occurred. The goal in this assessment exercise is to get a complete picture of your performance: how well you navigated in these various roles, and what barriers, both internal and external, may have existed to block your success. It would also be helpful if you considered any lessons learned.

What's the point of this exercise? We tend to be successful when we engage in activities that we enjoy and that we're good at. We tend to fail when we're feeling incompetent, don't understand some of the essential rules for success in an organization, or find ourselves in a role that we're not well suited for. The take-away: to identify key themes that have enabled us to achieve success and then to use these themes as a basis for identifying new roles where these themes will have the potential to be expressed. Alternatively, you may find that you're already on the right track. Then this exercise just serves as an important reminder about the strength of your convictions and the power of self-knowledge to achieve success.

> Andre and I met shortly after he graduated from Wharton. In 1997, an MBA from a top school combined with a CPA and CFA should have guaranteed him multiple offers from which to choose. He had only one, and it was with a second-tier foreign bank in a corporate lending training program. It happened late in his last semester after he had exhausted all his other on-campus recruiting options.
>
> The problem for Andre was this: He wanted a position in institutional sales. He was therefore competing against students who were less technically proficient but light years beyond him with respect to social skills and comfort with clients and colleagues. Andre had always relied on his analytical abilities to distinguish him and to excel, but they were less relevant in sales. Candidates needed to be smart, yes...but brilliant, no.
>
> Andre came to me after his first year at the bank. He was miserable. He felt that he failed back at school, but that he deserved another shot. He was determined to cross over to institutional sales at a top-tier institution. Good luck! He's a great guy, but you'd never describe him as a people person. We worked together on developing a strategy for the search and then preparing him for his interviews. It was all about a smart sell. That was our theme...to show that he was different but in a good way. He would market more complex institutional products and translate their benefits to a less-sophisticated client base. It worked. Andre got his first job. It lasted for a year or so. He could sell, but not enough, and the kind of sale he made took far too long to close. This theme repeated itself again and again and again. Yes, four moves in eight years.
>
> I had known for a long time that Andre needed to be in a role where his success would be tied directly to his analytical talents. It took him several years to reach this conclusion, however. Even as a mediocre salesperson, he was highly compensated compared to the rest of the world. We looked at all of his jobs, and it was obvious. He did not like to sell; he

liked to explain. He wanted to protect his clients and help them to be smarter. He wanted them to feel safe and secure and to know that they had made the very best possible decisions based upon his recommendations. What was our strategy for his job search? Yes, you guessed it...to pursue a buy-side analyst position evaluating alternative investments.

Interpreting This Information

Armed with all of this assessment information, what do you do with it? I'm also guessing that you may have at prior points in time engaged in other assessment activities and collected useful information elsewhere...more is always better. There are many, many approaches to organizing and sorting through this mass of material. Remember, your goal is to identify targets that will serve as drivers for your search. Please also remember a point I made earlier: No single strategy is guaranteed to produce insight. It's cumulative. Many exercises have the potential to produce many more moments of insight.

A Career Coach

The easiest and most direct approach to assessment is to work with a career counselor or career coach—I'll use both terms interchangeably. I am not recommending a life coach or a therapist. They can be helpful and important, but they'll be less likely to understand the kinds of options that are available to you or how to best market yourself in a world and industry that may be unfamiliar to them. When it comes to career counselors, not all are created equal. The shortest distance between two points may be a straight line, but when there's a problem with the tool you use to measure, you can end up going around in circles. That can be the difference between good and incompetent career support.

If you decide that you want to work with a coach, know that there's an expense involved. The rule of thumb: Experienced coaches charge more. Successful coaches charge more. Busy coaches charge more. Those who specialize in more complex career matters and who work with clients who are higher up in the food chain charge a lot more.

A high price tag, however, doesn't guarantee that you've made the right choice. The best strategy is to assemble a short list of coaches who have been recommended to you. Ask friends who are successful, friends who have recently been in search and landed, and get referrals from alumni and professional organizations like the CFA Institute. As you gather this information, find out about rates and fee structure. Never, ever commit to work with a coach where you pay a large fee upfront. Just like you and I can get fired, you deserve the right to fire your career coach if the relationship is not working out. It's very difficult to get a refund when the money has already been spent. On the other hand, also remember that career coaching and job search are not a science, so you may experience some frustration in any relationship you establish, even one that is highly productive.

Make a short list of three or four coaches to start and prepare a list of questions to ask, as follows:

1. Can you tell me about your approach?

   How do they work; what's their style? You need to figure out if their style is in sync with your ability to learn from them. Pay particular attention to the language they use. Is it conceptual or concrete? Which do you prefer and need as a client?

2. How does this process work?

   Are they able to explain simply and directly what to expect and whether your situation may warrant an alternative approach? Does it sound like the process is formulaic? Time-tested is good; putting you in a box is bad.

3. How long have you been doing this?

   You need to know how experienced they are. If you're going to place yourself, your career, and your trust in the hands of a relative novice, know that there's some risk.

4. How and when did you become a coach? Why?

This is actually a great question—or at least, I believe it is. Don't you want to know that your partner in this process has a good and meaningful reason to be advising you?

5. Can you tell me about a client you worked with where the process failed?

You should expect your coach to communicate openly and thoughtfully and to have insight into both successes and failures.

Please, never ask how long the process will take. I know there may be some stress around the expense and financial commitment. Your coach is not a fortune teller, and the market is more complicated than ever before. If he or she can tell you precisely how long this process will take, find another coach. It is impossible to predict the future. You will waste your time and money.

Last, but not least, if you still need a little more reassurance, ask your coach for references. Just one or two, and they should be appropriate to the kind of search you'll be engaged in. Of course, the coach will provide satisfied clients. It's still valuable to have their perspective as a consumer of the service.

Plug and Play

If a career coach is not an option or you want to supplement your work with the coach, this next strategy may offer interesting potential. At this point, you've collected a vast amount of information about yourself through the assessment exercises; now we take this information and begin to process it. Key themes have most likely emerged: You now have critical information about your skills, interests, values, and experience. As you organize the results, you'll begin to recognize patterns regarding subject matter and function as well as activities you enjoy.

This is exactly what happened to Rob, our trader turned fundraiser. We made a list of all the language and vocabulary that seemed most prominent and was often repeated in his assessments. This list included words and phrases such as the following:

- Fundraising
- Sales
- Client relationship management
- Marketing
- Not-for-profit
- Education
- Philanthropy

We took these words and plugged them into a few job posting boards. It didn't matter where the positions were located, so we ignored geography. The bigger the universe, the more options will surface that incorporate each of these fields. We got text rich job descriptions; profiles of positions that seemed to be appropriate based entirely on the number of shared matches. Yes, it's as simple as that.

Rob used these job postings to further define and direct his job search. In his networking conversations, he was able to explain with conviction and clarity what he wanted to do and why he was qualified. He could be even more specific in requesting information and ideas that would provide introductions to the right people and to the right organizations. He had the language now to explain himself, and he used this information in creating a resume that would support his job search. Easy!

Job Search Team

Let's return to the example of our friend, Maria, the international banker. She was determined to take her time and avoid making an impulsive move into the next situation, despite her fears of being out of the industry. She had made that mistake before—the consequences of which were damaging both professionally and personally. The challenge for her and for many of you who work on Wall Street is to manage the "gap"—the time between jobs when you're on the bench not by your choice, but as a result of a decision made by others. It's an involuntary sabbatical, and the prevailing belief is that it's bad...very bad. It's time not accounted for. Do I agree? No.

Maria was particularly sensitive to being viewed as "damaged goods." If you were so good, how could your firm have dismissed you? This is not a logical reaction to job loss in a market like ours, but it is a human and very natural reaction among highly competitive job seekers. Maria had never failed. She viewed not only her job loss but the time off, too, as signs of this failure. How to address the gap is the subject of several other chapters: interviews, strategy, and follow-up. For right now, my goal is to offer you a technique to use to keep you on track and to also help you establish and refine your focus.

I call it the Job Search Team. It's a group of like-minded people who you respect and who share a common goal: to either get a job or to stay employed. In Maria's case, she needed support on several levels. After losing her job, she felt demoralized and humiliated. She was uncomfortable being out among professional friends, and she had great difficulty explaining both the separation and what she wanted going forward. She was stuck.

Through word of mouth and her MBA alumni association, Maria identified six other individuals in search. Although it doesn't really matter much from my perspective, none were in the same area as Maria. She felt that having an additional level of competition among team members would be unproductive. I allowed her this. In truth, we live in a large world with very little control over events and opportunities. Why not share both the information and the strategies, and leave it up to the hiring manager to make the final decision as to the better fit? Besides, Maria wasn't clear yet on what direction she would pursue.

As a first introductory step, Maria and her fellow team members each prepared a brief bullet point summary highlighting their experience, skills, interests, values, likes, dislikes, and any other information that they were comfortable sharing. In Maria's case, we used this "profile" as a basis for getting feedback from fellow team members for the purposes of assessment. Although all the team members knew that it was Maria's profile they were analyzing, the intention was to remove as much personality as possible. It was also important to convey that all feedback would be gratefully and non-defensively accepted...no debates or arguments, but just a need for clarification. I encouraged Maria to ask them the following questions:

- In reading the profile of this individual, what sorts of career options or jobs come immediately to mind? Why?
- What do you see this person not being a good fit for? Why?
- Are there any people you know with this particular profile or one that closely resembles it? What sorts of jobs do these people have?

The goal here is to get smart people to think for you. It's a brainstorming exercise. The more options the team identifies, the better. In Maria's case, the team produced four job ideas that felt right to her. It was up to Maria then to explore each.

As I mentioned a moment ago, Maria needed support on several levels. She was unclear about the next step, but she also needed to protect herself from some potentially very bad habits. Maria relies heavily on external structure and feedback as a motivator for accomplishment. Without the benefit of an organization to evaluate her, she was at a loss to maintain a high level of self motivation. It worked when she had an interview, but those felt like sprints to her. She needed a consistent and regular source of support and regular reporting on her progress. Meeting weekly gave her a deadline and a standard by which to measure her progress.

Last but not least, the team served as a resource for generating ideas and providing a nice blend of unconditional support and tough love. It allowed Maria to practice and experiment with her job search in the safety of a trusted group. They still meet today. All members have found jobs, lost jobs, and relied heavily on the feedback of other members for managing challenging situations on the job.

Assessment Strategy

When it comes to assessment, remember that patience is a virtue—and so is persistence. Unless you're unusually lucky right out of the gate, or you already know what you want to do, please take the time to complete these exercises. Then share this information with the right people; people who can offer insight and encouragement. It's time consuming and tedious, but the results can be incredibly powerful. You've seen how this process works through the various client stories I've shared. Not all of them began with a systematic and thoughtful strategy. When that happens, there's always a need to back track. Why make the same mistake?

4

Stick the Landing: How to Move Successfully from the Sell-Side to the Buy-Side

For years, clients have approached me to help them make the transition from the sell-side to the buy-side. They come from a range of functions and organizations. They're traders, institutional salespeople, or analysts in equity or fixed income research. They also tend to be consistent in why they want to make the move. Their reasons shouldn't surprise you: Clients cite quality of life, less politics, smaller firms, equity ownership, and "pay-out" to list a few.

Most professionals in the securities and financial services industry believe that buy-side firms such as hedge funds tie performance directly to the P&L. So, if your firm is making investment decisions based on your advice, and you've made great calls, then the upside potential is vast. On the other hand, that may also explain why some analysts stay on the sell-side or others decide to return there. A few bad calls that blow up won't necessarily get you fired. There's safety in numbers.

In truth, the move is not a difficult one to explain or to understand. The buy-side has long been a desirable destination. It's intuitively obvious...most professionals on Wall Street want to work where decisions are driven by the investors, not by the investment bankers. On the sell-side, research is a cost center. It's paid for through commissions earned by traders, so there's a need to always justify your existence if you're in research. When your performance is measured subjectively, you're always at the mercy and kindness of your revenue-generating colleagues. Face it—you're their bitch.

It's not so much the destination that matters in making this transition a success—the options include hedge funds, private equity firms, insurance companies, and investment managers—it's how you get there that seems to be the biggest hurdle. In most cases, professionals ready to make the leap already know what they want, they have a pretty good idea why, and they're ready. Clients seem to always get stuck around the same inflection point: figuring out how to actually execute the search. In other words, how do you go from a great idea to a real job and then to an actual offer?

Making any move these days is tough enough. Why is it that a move from the sell-side to the buy-side presents additional challenges? It has to! There are fewer options and opportunities nowadays. Hundreds of hedge funds have disappeared, which swells the supply of qualified and available candidates with directly related experience. Several investment banks have also folded or merged. Again, that represents another pipeline for experienced people.

The process for crossing over, as with much of job search, is surprisingly uncomplicated. It's the execution that presents the greatest challenges. If that's the case, please pay particular attention to events and moods that have the potential to be disruptive and get you off track. It's inevitable that a challenging job search will produce highs and lows, especially in a market with many more candidates than available positions and in a function that is highly desirable. You cannot afford to take it personally. Evaluate any and all feedback you receive and incorporate only those elements that make you a stronger and more attractive candidate. Discard immediately discouraging feedback not replicated through additional reality testing. If it's real and meaningful, you have no choice but to pay attention. On the other hand, negative feedback may be just one person's unique and possibly soured view of the world.

To illustrate from personal experience, I made the decision in 1989 to transition to the outplacement industry, an industry that many of you may have experienced firsthand. It seemed like the perfect fit for an ex-banker and career counselor: working with executives who were being involuntarily separated from their firms and receiving formalized job search assistance.

I began to network, which was a brand-new concept for me, and I was introduced to the fellow running the New York office of one of the world's leading firms at the time and today, too. Doug's advice, may he rest in peace, was unexpected: Outplacement is a dying industry. That was not what I wanted to hear, and it certainly didn't correspond with my own understanding of the changing nature of work and careers. Of course, I took his perspective into account, but I didn't let it or him discourage me from pursuing my goal. I used it as a reality check in other conversations and also as a motivating force. I didn't agree with Doug, and I was going to prove him wrong. I knew it had to be wrong based both on my own intuition and my expectations for how the world of work and career were evolving. And years later, it is now an anecdote.

In this situation, we can't offer a trusted roadmap others have used. The approach varies from person to person depending upon their experience and niche in the industry. Still, we can learn practices and benchmarks that assure us we're moving in the right direction. At first, adopt a linear approach. Identify your target and proceed. Network, respond to postings, and contact companies directly. Notice that I've omitted recruiters from the list. Generally, recruiters are only paid to deliver a perfect match. That's not you yet. Don't eliminate them from the mix, but don't rely on them either. As a candidate, you may be passionate about the target, but that's not enough for a recruiter to earn his or her fee. As your search unfolds, it will eventually involve many more elements: organizations, people, and ideas. That's your goal: to achieve a dynamic multi-faceted state with a lot of moving parts. A plan helps you to organize, keep track of, and make sure important matters do not slip through your fingers.

Five Steps to a Perfect Landing

Develop a Game Plan

The process is pretty simple. Depending on where you want to go on the buy-side, you need a strategy to position yourself. The first step is to make sure that you're clear on the target. What specifically do you envision for yourself? Why? Is it a defensible strategy? Does it all make sense? Is it obvious based on how you've structured the story you tell people?

The game plan is organized as follows:

- **Firming up the target.**   In making a move like this, your audience needs to feel like they are the center of your universe. Unlike other searches in a tough market where it's practical to have a few related options, this is the exception to the "flake" rule.

- **Ask "why?"**   When a target is highly competitive, you need good reasons to support both why it's desirable to you and why you're qualified. Alternatively, ask "why not?" It's a big world. There should be more than enough opportunities to go around if you're creative, energetic, and thick-skinned.

- **Fine-tune the resume.**   The resume and any additional materials to support how and why you're pursuing this target all need to be aligned. Does it all make sense? Is there a consistency, logic, and flow? Remember, you can't re-write your history, but it can be presented in a way that minimizes distraction and maximizes the message that you're serious about pursuing this goal.

- **The story: your value and your value proposition.**   When you talk about yourself and the reasons for "crossing over," here's where you begin to weave together your experience, your qualifications, and the "why's." This is an explanation that is both historical and focused on the future. Your past must naturally support the decision. Equally important, you need to show that your potential to contribute is untapped and ever expanding. So...your value is measured by the benefits both immediate and over the longer term that you produce. Your value proposition is the story you tell to demonstrate why it's a no brainer for you to make the move. You'll also be taken more seriously.

Know the Universe

If you're clear on your goal, then you better be clear on where you want to work. Research and knowledge are critical. Make a comprehensive list of companies where you have the potential to be a candidate. It's a starting point. Whether or not an opportunity exists is irrelevant. The goal is to know who you could work for. This list should expand as your search continues for two important reasons, as follows:

- If you want to be taken seriously, you need to know what the market looks like and how the various firms are alike and different. This makes you sound like you're smart. It also serves as a valuable resource in your meetings. You can share knowledge that you've acquired about the competition. People like to know what other people are up to. It also presents you as more of an insider.
- You should not expect any single conversation or meeting to produce an offer. In fact, as you network with people in positions that you would like for yourself, they will most likely not have positions at their firms. What they will have is information about the industry, and if you make a good impression, the commitment to provide names of other people to speak to and referrals if they hear of opportunities.

Distinguish Yourself from the Competition

You need to position yourself against other candidates and professionals who already work on the buy-side. In a tougher market, your competition will be candidates like you who want to cross over and those who already have this experience. A lot of those folks have been displaced. This requires demonstrating your immediate and long-term value to the prospective firm: When an employer evaluates you, he or she will be thinking—revenue, results, and good numbers.

How do you reposition yourself?

- **Conduct a dynamic search.** You demonstrate your capacity for success by showing the relevance in what you've already done and by how well you've performed. People hire people who have the potential to add value immediately. You also need to kiss a lot of frogs in this process. That's the volume part. You never know which conversations and meetings will lead to the Holy Grail—your new job.

- **Passion, enthusiasm, and determination.** You bring a fresh new perspective. You need to imply this in how you present yourself: Why hire a "re-tread," someone who may have a mediocre track record and performance? You, on the other hand, have a perfectly legitimate explanation for being on the market, available, and wanting to make a change: The sell-side is hemorrhaging, and you have long considered this a destination. This is never stated explicitly—that would be dangerous. Note to buy-side readers: All's fair in love and job search. When you interview, the theme is: Why would you ever consider someone without direct experience when they can get a candidate of your caliber?

- **The right collateral materials.** As a candidate crossing over, you need to go above and beyond to demonstrate your commitment and desire to make a change. Nothing less is acceptable. All the materials you present must show both your understanding of the subject matter and your ability to skill-fully weave in the message of this new and logical next step in your career. That's true for your resume and all correspondence.

Identify Common Barriers and Issues

Are you aware of the prevailing beliefs and myths about differences between the buy-side and sell-side? These will surface in how you present yourself and in how you address one of the biggest challenges in making the transition: what may be viewed as an apparent lack of depth. Some of the more common themes include the following:

- Sell-side research is a cost center paid for by trading commissions. That means the traders call the shots.

- The sell-side often produces long reports. Translate: You should like to write, you need to be fast, and you have to be good.

- On the buy-side, your performance is tied to the P&L. That's potentially lucrative over the long term if you work your way up the food chain from being an analyst to running your own money.

- Yes, the upside potential at hedge funds is vast.

- You make great calls, you make great money. It's easier on the buy-side to correlate performance when your firm is investing off your advice.

- The inverse (and not necessarily true, but expressed by a few of my buy-side clients): Analysts stay on the sell-side because it's safer. You're less likely to get blown up by making a few bad calls.

When you anticipate reasonable challenges, whether they're myth or reality-based, you have a better handle on how to present yourself. It's not enough to convey your knowledge. You have to insist that the transition is seamless. There's a big difference between the following statements:

- I have substantial experience as a sell-side trader. I also recently completed my CFA.

- In my capacity as a sell-side trader, I've always been extremely rigorous in analyzing the securities I've traded. Because I enjoy that part of the process so much, I decided to complete the CFA designation. That was a great experience; I learned a lot, and it re-confirmed my desire to move over to the buy-side.

The first is a statement of fact. It leads you nowhere. The second translates and justifies.

Focus

Based upon my experience, even when the first four steps are in place, the process will break down unless there is a sustained commitment to achieving your goal. It's very easy for smart people to get distracted. In fact, smart people are more likely to get discouraged. They rely heavily on positive feedback for motivation and that's generally not forthcoming when you're in search.

Moving to the buy-side is not a standard issue job search. Conducting a search that involves many moving parts—re-positioning yourself, justifying the move, preparing the collateral materials, producing meaningful following-up—is a lot like running a marathon. It will require a monumental effort. It will also require considerable discipline and focus. You may know that the decision to move to the buy-side is obvious and right, but there are a lot of skeptics out there who will still need to be convinced. If you're easily discouraged, then you'll need to be mindful of your potential to get derailed as this process unfolds. The real question is: Do you want to make this happen? If so, how important is it to you? What will you do to avoid the distractions that you and I can easily enumerate? And when they do surface, how will you minimize them?

Jean Pierre: Getting Back on Track... a New One

When I met Jean Pierre (let's call him JP), he had recently finalized his divorce. It was not an amicable separation. In other words, he got hosed. He was out of work, broke, already behind in his alimony payments, and due to a complex custody agreement, limited in his ability to re-locate. The situation was serious.

JP was a sell-side trader in his late 30's. He was downsized from a large brokerage firm and had been out now for about six months. During the final months at work, he was distracted by the divorce, and as a result, his performance suffered. When we sat down for our first conversation, he was a mess, both physically and emotionally. He had apparently gained upwards of 50 pounds, he was discouraged, and he felt stuck.

First step: We established a target. What kind of job did JP want? Ideally, he was hoping to eventually become a portfolio manager. That was a target, yes. But clearly it could not be accomplished immediately. JP got himself into this mess. It would take some effort to get him out. Sometimes when clients make the decision to finally meet with a career coach, they think the coach will have all the answers and the potential to quickly make something happen that they couldn't. That's not the way it works. Realistic expectations combined with a thoughtful and carefully planned strategy produce results. That's the role of the coach. There is no magic in this process.

JP's target for the time being was to find another trading position either on the buy-side or sell-side. For right now, it didn't matter which. Our goal was to get him back to work as quickly as possible and to begin to restore a damaged reputation. I felt strongly that his priority should be a job and that the longer term and more challenging goal would be much easier to achieve with a paycheck. Once he got a job, any job, we'd deal with the "what next"? For now, we focused on how to present his story:

> I left the bank about six months ago. I had a long and, from most reports, distinguished track record there. The bank was really good to me...but I knew that I was in a vulnerable position when the rumors began to circulate about potential layoffs. In fact, it seemed kind of obvious to me that I'd be on the short list. I was going through the final stages of a difficult divorce. I was distracted, and my performance in my last few months there suffered. I know it, my boss was aware of the situation, but it is what it is.
>
> My goal now is to find a trading position either on the sell-side or with a hedge fund.

Notice that JP wove in some personal information. Under most circumstances, that's not a strategy I recommend...unless not weaving it in makes for an even more challenging story to tell. In JP's case, it worked to his advantage to provide some context. Without a little background and just a bit of drama, there are too many unanswered questions. Besides, what he went through would probably resonate with many of the people he was meeting with. A personal trauma like a divorce after many years of marriage would position the last few months before to his separation, explain the mediocre performance, and justify the time off since leaving work.

It wasn't that different from another client of mine who happened to have a devastating fire around the time of her separation from her job as an investment banker. In an interview, discussion of events like these offers an interesting and distracting story. More important, they will satisfy the need of most compassionate people that what you've told them is both true and that you left your job for the right reasons. If you're likely to be derailed by rejection, keep in mind that most people will show some level of kindness and understanding. Others won't buy it. They'll dismiss you or what you've told them as frivolous, a sign of weakness, or irrelevant. So be it. Job search is about managing rejection.

I encouraged JP to consider an interim position on the sell-side. One of these options—selling bonds on a commission basis—represented low-hanging fruit. It was accessible and easier to secure. Although the role was not desirable to JP longer term, the barriers to entry were minimal. He'd been out for a while, and I didn't want him to lose track of what was happening in the market. It wasn't where he wanted to be, but it was one step closer to being back at work. We could easily modify the story to reflect wherever he landed.

> I made the decision to return to work as quickly as possible once I resolved all of the issues around the divorce. It wasn't an ideal situation. I knew that going in, and I was willing to make the trade-off. I wanted and needed to be making money. My long-term goal is to move to the buy-side. That's why I'm here meeting with you.

As long as JP was re-settled in a new position, he was ready to begin the next round of job search. It's easy enough to explain a decision to compromise—most people have or will at some point in their careers. For JP, the decision to join and then to leave all gets woven seamlessly into the story.

Dan: Sell-Side Hopper

Dan is the kind of guy who should have always worked on the buy-side. It was obvious to just about everyone except to him. As an accountant between undergraduate and law school, he was drawn to the most complex accounting matters. Derivatives were relatively new, and Dan immediately found himself assigned to the firm's banking clients. You would have thought an MBA was the next step. Instead, Dan felt strongly that a BS in business was sufficient and that the law would offer valuable structure and discipline. He was also interested in serving as a legal advisor on capital markets transactions...or so he thought.

Law school was a disaster from the start. Dan performed well academically. It was just a bad fit. His first summer at a law firm confirmed that he was on the wrong track. His second summer at a bank got him re-energized and excited about his career. He was able to audit classes at the university's business school, and upon graduation, he joined a commercial bank in its swaps group.

Dan remained with the bank for a couple of years and continued to market swaps to corporate clients. He performed well there and eventually he was promoted to Managing Director. Dan wasn't rewarded for his skill as a marketer. He fit the bank's culture, which valued and nurtured its intellectual capital. He loved to translate these complex new instruments to a relatively unsophisticated client base. He was good at it. He could make what was dense and technical seem easy and obvious. It was like a puzzle to him. Along the way, he prepared for and received his CFA designation. He felt that the technical knowledge and financial analysis would be a nice complement to his legal degree. It would also demonstrate that his loyalty was not to the law but to pursuing a career in finance.

Dan was recruited to join a top investment bank to sell derivatives. Quite frankly, it was an opportunity he could not ignore. He would receive an enormous guarantee for the first year, a decent sign-on to offset the bonus he left on the table at the bank and to equalize his lost stock options, the MD title, and the potential to earn vast sums of money. Dan and I met around this time, and we worked together on the negotiation strategy.

Dan knew that he made the wrong decision almost immediately. His boss wanted him to sell hard to every potential customer, regardless of need. Dan got his motivation from the more difficult transactions. He didn't sell. That's not how he viewed himself. He much preferred to explain and to translate. It was an unhappy, brief marriage on both sides followed by a quick divorce. A few months into the job, Dan was asked to leave. Naturally, he was paid out for the year but that still left him feeling empty, humiliated, and confused. He was perplexed as to how the process unfolded and where he fell short. He was even more concerned as to how to explain the separation and how to re-emerge.

It was the first time Dan failed professionally, and he was devastated. He'd show them. He'd be back in the market soon and win. It was obvious to everyone, including Dan, that there was not a snowball's chance in hell that he and the firm could have ever been even remotely compatible with respect to business development and revenue generation. Despite this knowledge, Dan was motivated by revenge and rage. **FACT:** That's not generally a good starting point for success in career management. It may get you a job quickly but not necessarily the right job.

It was a buyer's market at the time, so the story we prepared to explain Dan's very short and highly conspicuous tenure was not that challenging to tell. Besides, Dan had an almost flawless track record. His career, reputation, and performance at the commercial bank were strong enough to neutralize the fallout from his recent involuntary separation. It had to be. His U-5, the uniform termination record for registered securities industry professionals, reported the termination as performance-related.

I suggested to Dan that his personality might be better suited for a career on the buy-side as an analyst, with the goal over time of becoming a portfolio manager.

> No, I like sales, I'm good at it with the right support in place [or so he thought], and I want to focus on earning as much money as I can.

If only Dan had taken some time off to consider his options. Instead, we prepared his explanation. He was eager to get started:

> I was recruited aggressively to join the bank. I wasn't actively looking at the time. They presented a package that I couldn't pass up...which should have been an early warning to me that this was not going to be the right environment. Initially, I was not going to leave my job but they came back with an offer that just blew me away. We agreed on a reasonable time frame for me to come up to speed, but with changes in management, there didn't seem to be a commitment to my success.

If there's additional information that provides important context, please use it to your advantage. Not to express anger—just to provide information that will help the person interviewing you better understand why and how the separation occurred. For example, Dan might add, if true:

> There'd been some turnover in management. I had a three-month non-compete in place. So, by the time I actually joined the team, it looked a lot different than when the offer was extended.

Dan received several offers. Naturally, he chose a position similar to the one he recently lost. He joined a large global investment bank selling structured products. Revenge may be sweet for the moment, but over the long term, it may prove to be impractical.

Dan's next job lasted for a couple of years. He seemed to survive in the new firm just barely and only by the skin of his teeth. Being smart helped and so did a few longstanding, loyal client relationships. He was never considered a star, and most often he felt like he was invisible. It was like dying a slow death. In large part, the majority of his conversations with senior management were one-sided and usually focused on weaknesses in his performance. When the mandate is to sell, and you see yourself as an analyst and as a relationship manager, you've got a problem. Organizations don't like contradictions, and Dan finally began to understand that his profile was unsuited for the role he was playing.

Dan needed a kick in the pants. That happened when he was called into a meeting with his boss and HR. Technically speaking, he wasn't being fired. It was a performance warning. He was offered two options: either take a package now, or try to improve his numbers within three months. In general, they don't really want you to succeed. They've already made the decision, and that's why the targets that are set for you are virtually impossible to achieve. Their goal is to avoid potential litigation and to appear benevolent. Suspecting this, Dan chose the latter. When you're faced with a decision like Dan's, my recommendation is to take the one that buys you as much time as you can possibly squeeze out of them. Job search is always easier to explain while you have a job or at least the pretense of one.

Dan met with me to determine how to best position the separation. **Correction:** He was not yet officially separated! He was still gainfully and productively employed. The decision to leave, for right now, was his. In a situation like this—when you've bought yourself more time—please don't complicate the explanation by introducing unnecessary information before it needs to be. It will add a dimension to your story that I guarantee will raise questions you shouldn't and don't need to be asked yet. For the time being, here's how Dan explained his desire to shift the focus of his career. Bear in mind the following:

- He'd be speaking to a skeptical or possibly resentful audience: *You guys on the sell-side are paid far too much and I'm just as smart as you. What's really behind your decision to switch?* Remember, Dan moved twice after the swaps position, both for sales roles and both to follow the money.

- He needed a story that would be comprehensive but not be a burden to digest.
- There were many qualified candidates out there with recent and relevant experience. What would make Dan a better, stronger, and more valuable candidate?
- Initially, Dan's only goal was to get meetings and to expand his universe of contacts on the buy-side. He was not ready yet to present himself as a candidate. He didn't know enough about the role or have the confidence to present his ideas with real conviction and authority.

I'm really grateful that you've agreed to spend time with me. Thank you.

Let me explain to you why I'm here. Briefly, I've made the decision to shift the direction of my career from institutional sales to buy-side analysis. Long term, I'd like to be a portfolio manager. It's a decision that I've given a lot of thought to over the years, and I figure, you just go around once. I've been on a track, and although I've been doing well, it's not what I enjoy most. I've always been drawn to more complex analysis, and that's how I've distinguished my work with clients.

Having a law degree, I'm very comfortable with researching, gathering, and presenting information. Getting the CFA designation, which I did in three years, gives me the subject matter expertise, and also a lot more depth as an analyst.

I realize that there are a lot of qualified people out there. I figure it's only a matter of time, hard work, and many, many conversations with experts like you. So...I'm open to any advice you have on how I can best position myself. I'd also appreciate recommendations on firms I should target and other people I should talk to.

I know—the explanation is a little long. Dan had the option of presenting it in its entirety or breaking it down depending on the mood and tone of the meeting. It's important to be mindful that the people you're networking with may be very busy, and they may also have a short attention span when it comes to your interests and goals.

Dan discovered that having a good story was not enough. He was missing a competitive advantage—a compelling reason to be taken seriously in a very tough market. Lots of other people had good stories, too. In meeting after networking meeting, one theme was raised again and again: *We know you're smart, and we know that you want to make this move. What we don't know is why we would select you over someone else.* It was a powerful message that Dan could not ignore.

What was missing? In a word, proof. He had not yet demonstrated his ability to actually perform the analysis that would be central to his new career goal. Probably more important, he had not demonstrated that he was willing to go above and beyond to make this happen. Dan needed to address all skeptics head on, the people who were thinking: *Yes, we know you want this. But so what!* Our strategy: Dan identified two companies with interesting financials, and he prepared reports on each. These reports became his calling card and a primary reason to network.

> I've made the decision to shift the focus of my career from institutional sales to an analyst role on the buy-side. I've prepared analyses of two companies, company A and B, and I'd be grateful for your feedback. [Dan found after several meetings that one company analysis was enough to pique interest; two was a little overwhelming.] If I'm going to make this move, I need to show people that I can actually do the work, not just say it, and that I have the potential to contribute immediately.

> Later in the conversation:

> Do you have any recommendations of firms and people I should approach? Would you be willing to make an introduction?

Our strategy for Dan's job search worked. We were able to show the analysts and portfolio managers he was networking with the quality of his work, demonstrate his willingness to go the extra mile to pursue his goal, and to lock them in. These were very busy people. We knew that once Dan got their feedback, advice, and respect, in large part, they'd be hooked. They invested time in him, and now they would want him to succeed.

Debbie: Buy-Side to Sell-Side

Debbie got off to a slow start following graduation from Notre Dame. Despite the fact that she graduated almost at the top of her class, she was uninformed about job search and uncomfortable in her interviews. It was also a tough market for college grads, and she was not coming from a top school where Wall Street firms typically recruit. After working as a waitress and property manager for almost two years, she was finally successful in securing an entry-level position in high-yield research for a large overseas bank. It helped that she completed levels one and two of the CFA exam and that she was preparing for level three. For Debbie, she had reached a critical turning point—she had her first job in her industry.

Debbie was promoted from Analyst to Associate in 16 months. A year later, she was recruited aggressively to join a family office doing distressed research. She wasn't looking; a call came in from a recruiter who convinced her to have an initial meeting. It couldn't hurt, right? In fact, it was an opportunity she couldn't pass up: co-managing a $1+ billion multi strategy fund and also reporting directly to the portfolio manager responsible for managing a large distressed debt fund. He was a fellow with a great reputation, and he seemed like a nice guy, too. In addition to a big bump in pay, Debbie finally found her way to her version of Oz: New York City. It was a lifelong dream finally made real.

Just around the time of Debbie's first-year anniversary, her boss departed unexpectedly. He apparently had ongoing disagreements with the family on investment strategy. Although she had a vague awareness that some tension existed, it never occurred to her that he might be fired. It was so sudden, and it felt wrong. She realized that her boss had shielded her from the day-to-day political issues and much of the dysfunction of the family. Debbie immediately felt vulnerable. A new boss would be joining shortly. It was very likely that he would recruit his own team. She made a couple of calls to recruiters, and within three or four weeks, she had two offers, both newly established hedge funds. She joined the larger of the two as a fundamental credit analyst. The head of the family office tried to convince her to stay, but Debbie had already made her decision. She felt that the relationship was now damaged beyond repair.

Fast forward six months: The hedge fund that Debbie joined had trouble raising money for its principal fund. Its performance was also mediocre. Recognizing that the situation was extremely serious and only getting worse, Debbie called the firm that made her the second offer. She transitioned seamlessly into a similar role. Then all hell broke loose. Less than a year after joining the firm, she and the rest of the team were dismissed: the market tanked, the hedge fund reported lousy earnings, and the redemptions had already begun. It was a mess, and Debbie felt that her career and life were spiraling out of control.

What was next for Debbie? Recruiters had all but disappeared, and those who returned her calls were either skeptical about the chain of events or their assignments, which were few and far between, were for highly specialized candidates. Nothing surfaced, and she was growing more and more discouraged. Debbie was referred to me by a colleague who she worked with at the bank and who I had also coached a while back. The bank seemed like a lifetime ago to Debbie. It was: Three jobs in less than four years.

Prior to our first meeting, Debbie and I spoke by phone. I asked her how long she'd been out—six months—and what she wanted. Silence for a moment or two. She seemed confused. Wasn't the answer obvious? Maybe her friend's advice to see me was not going to be helpful. Maybe it was a waste of money.

I'm looking for another analyst position at a hedge fund [YOU MORON!].

COACH: But hedge funds aren't hiring. Debbie, you need to expand your goal. It's just not large enough to support a robust search.

Wow, I was surprised that Debbie, an enormously accomplished analyst, would be so unaware. It's the old shoemaker's children proverb. She was a great evaluator of external matters—equities, companies, and industries—but she had little insight into her own career goals and talents. If that were all, it would have been a piece of cake; some work on our part to address the gaps but not an uncommon challenge. More pressing and serious, there seemed to be an unwillingness to demand what she wanted and needed to do to sustain her career.

COACH: Well, Debbie, you've worked on both the sell-side and the buy-side, and not for especially long in the latter area. Did you not enjoy your time at the bank?

DEBBIE: No, it was a really great entry job, and I did well there. I had a great boss. I also made a lot of good friends.

COACH: Why not explore options on both the buy-side and the sell-side? Let's expand your target.

DEBBIE: Could I go back?

COACH: Absolutely—as long as you have a good story to tell.

With a shrinking universe of firms, and most of those firms not hiring, Debbie had no choice but to expand her target. It became clear to me that she was approaching her career as a linear path...that what she did immediately prior would determine what options existed for her going forward. No, Debbie, it doesn't have to work that way if you look at your career collectively. Instead of presenting yourself as a hedge fund analyst, let's just call you an equities analyst, which is what you've always been. A minor change will rebrand you instantly and offer you greater versatility, too.

The challenge then was to find a way to weave together all of her experience, explain the moves and various decisions non-defensively, and clearly articulate her goal. That story would be a moving target. It was subject to change depending on whether conversations were with buy-side or sell-side people.

If Debbie is interviewing or networking with a person on the sell-side, here's what she might say:

> I'm an analyst. My decision to leave the bank was not intentional. It had absolutely nothing to do with wanting to work for a hedge fund or a family office. It was about the opportunity to acquire significant meaningful experience in bankruptcy and distressed. It was an amazing opportunity! Besides, having worked now for two hedge funds, I've discovered that there's a lot of unnecessary stress and drama related to the positions you take. There's often a fight to get them into the book, and then when a problem comes down, it's the "blame" game. My goal is to find a stable platform.

If Debbie is questioned further on what she means by a stable platform:

> Yes, I know there's the potential to make a lot of money in a bull market. On the other hand, when the market turns—which is inevitable—investors will pull out...so funding and volatility cannot be ignored.

It is not impossible to return to the sell-side. In Debbie's case, she was tired of being unemployed. Her explanation had to reflect two important themes:

- Functionally, she never left. She was, and will always be, an analyst.
- She gained valuable experience from each and every experience.

If you've made the decision to return, then you, too, need to figure out what your key themes will be to support the move. If the reasoning is weak, don't expect your audience to believe you.

5

The Art of the Bear Market Resume

You're managing your career in the securities industry in tough times...probably like no other downturn you've ever experienced. Even as the markets improve, the structural, economic, and political aftershocks of the economic calamity will keep job search very competitive for many years. Moods and expectations in finance ride the highs and lows of the markets, and even as overall trends improve, the markets will continue bouncing back and forth and back again. For the foreseeable future, these bounces can send your career and future into an unexpected direction. Your resume will cushion the fall only if it maximizes your attractiveness. That means a strong message and an equally powerful value proposition: what you want, what you offer, and why.

Most of you are connected 24/7. You work in environments that provide instant information and immediate feedback on your performance. Decisions about staffing and human resource matters are made with speed, efficiency, and not surprisingly, a lack of kindness. They're also generally made without a commitment to longer-term strategy. The globality, speed, and power of information and financial networks brought about a permanent shift in business leadership mindset. Corporate managers view results in data, profitability, and analytics—and no longer strongly associate people and relationships with those results. There is zero loyalty and even less gratitude.

Market melt-downs have become standard operating procedure, and the time between them has been compressed. As a result, Wall

Street firms hire, they fire, and people disappear. I know this and have seen it happen repeatedly. You probably know it firsthand, too. It's inevitable that you will lose your job and that you will also find yourself in job search. That means you always need to have an updated and targeted resume. It's what I refer to as a Bear Market resume principally because that's the market you're in. Of course, you'll need one in a Bull Market, too. It just doesn't have to be as good.

The art of the Bear Market resume lies in addressing three points clearly and precisely: what you want and why, what qualifies you to pursue this goal, and how the person reading the resume will benefit:

- **What do you want and why?**

  What's your goal? What do you want to be right now at this very moment in time? This is the central theme that should be conveyed loudly and forcefully from the top of your resume through the very last word.

  It's fine to have multiple goals. In fact, I encourage you to explore a range of options. However, your resume must be tightly focused around one major goal. Don't attempt to write a resume that positions you for a number of options. It's not a one-size-fits-all document. It can't be. In a competitive market—in any market for that matter—your resume is one more tool you use to establish your brand and your professional identity. A fuzzy message is the equivalent of resume suicide.

  How you distinguish yourself and present your experience and qualifications matters. If you don't figure out how to get your message across clearly, precisely, and with a bit of flair, someone else will. That doesn't mean every job requires a customized resume. That would be logistically challenging and unproductive. Part of being in job search is seeing some byproduct of the time you've invested in your search. How do you measure the success of your resume? When you send it out, you get calls. You should expect your resume to generate interest.

  The resume can encompass one or more related job categories. These are jobs that are similar in function, and they value, to a lesser or greater degree, the same qualifications, experience, and skills. If your goals are aligned with those of your target audience, then you've got a lovefest. Even in a tough market, your resume will generate real measurable interest. Remember that it's a marketing tool above and beyond all else. The broader the audience and the resume, the more likely your message will be diluted.

- **What qualifies you?**

Why do you deserve to present yourself as a candidate for this position? That's a question you better have a good answer to. Of course, you have to be convincing that you want it—passion is good—and that you have the brain-power to do the job. But it's not enough to show that you're smart. Smart people are not necessarily successful in job search. Your resume needs to take this insight to the next level and think for the reader.

It's your job to show your audience that who you say you are— your work experience, skills, qualifications, and interests— directly support what they, the audience, need and want. It should also imply that you, as presented via your resume, have the potential to offer something more: the answer. The people who interview you are working in increasingly complicated environments. They have the right to know that you will hit the ground running...immediately. You need to demonstrate that you will find solutions to problems that have not yet even been identified.

- **Benefits?**

What's in it for your reader? If you want to be taken seriously, the resume must always show that you have a history of adding value both immediately and over the longer term. Agreed— offering up solutions is a good way to demonstrate that value. The people who make hiring decisions will be grateful.

Before you sign off on the resume, however, there's one additional step to consider: how to measure your past performance. If your history is an indicator of your potential to be successful in the future, you have no choice but to provide metrics that quantify your value. For those of you in roles that are transaction-driven, it's easy to monetize your success. This is sometimes a challenge for my clients who work behind the scenes in functions such as back- or middle-office operations. Because their work is often not directly revenue generating, measuring success requires additional attention and creativity.

If that's the case, here are some questions to help you capture the results and outcomes of your work, whether it was administrative, project-based, or operational. When you describe the various projects you've worked on or the processes you've managed, consider the following:

- What did you do to manage this project or process in a new or better way?
- What lessons did you learn that have the potential to be replicated elsewhere?
- What were the results? Has your work contributed to the bottom-line? For example, even in roles that are administrative or operational, you can still achieve percentage increases in efficiency or productivity or reductions in overhead.

Preparing a Resume

When it comes to preparing your resume, there's no single format that will work in every situation. In general, the rule is: Less is more. Your resume should be written for the reader with a short attention span. That's the standard issue Wall Street trader type with "ADD." He or she will demand the following information from you: *Where* did you work, *what* were your responsibilities there, and *how well* did you perform? Any additional information has the potential to feel like a burden to this reader.

It's not about right or wrong or creating a perfect document. Your resume will not, and should never, be perfect. That's why this chapter is not particularly long. There's no incremental benefit for spending enormous amounts of time trying to outsmart the market. Besides, it's a moving target. As you proceed in job search, your resume must change as you gather new and important information to better position yourself. The goal is to get a majority of people who read your resume to agree that the message you're communicating is clear, powerful, and easy to digest. Unanimous approval is a waste of time and unproductive. Your theme should be: Is it good enough to get you out there and to generate interest?

Resume length is a subject that seems to get a lot of unnecessary attention. How long: one, two, or three pages? It doesn't really matter. The goal is to get the reader to pay attention from the very top of the resume and to want to read it through to the end. In theory, then, a good resume could be 100 pages...as long as your audience is willing to read it. What will make a difference?

- Knowing the prevailing resume strategy for the kind of position you're seeking. If your audience is made up primarily of traders, they will barely tolerate one page.

- Creating a resume that is appropriate for the level of position you see yourself in. A very senior position deserves a big resume. Holding back is a potential liability. Your reader wants to know that you have the breadth of experience and confidence to assume a position that others shouldn't. And the only way to convey that you're not a stretch for the position is to show it through language and illustration. Your audience needs this information to be sure that you're the right person.

- Getting your message across with excitement and passion. Wordiness without direction is the kiss of death. It will kill your resume. If you're going to tell a story, make sure it's readable.

The Summary Statement

The summary is the foundation for your entire search. A good summary anchors your message for the reader. It gives your reader a way to get what you're all about quickly. Here's an exception to the summary rule. If it's obvious from the body of your resume what you want to do—your experience is immediately self-explanatory to the reader, and it's presented in a way that gets that same reader excited—then there's absolutely no reason to use a summary. It's redundant. You also need to be mindful of readers with short attention span, like traders. If you've always been what you want and expect to be, and it's obvious from the resume, skip the summary. It just takes up valuable shelf space.

You use a summary when something needs to be explained, such as the following:

- You're making a career change.
- You've moved around enough to require an explanation as a prophylactic measure.
- You've moved in a direction that may need to be explained. For example, you took a job because you needed one, not because it was the right job.
- You have the right experience, but that experience on its own feels lifeless. The summary will give your resume a little punch.

Most summary statements tend to provide information in a general non-specific format. That's not my approach. I prefer messages that go somewhere—messages that explain what you want, what qualifies you, and how good you are. Effective messages don't use language that's generic. If the point of a resume is to distinguish you from other candidates, why use tired, familiar words and ideas to describe yourself? Some language is obvious and adds no meaning: senior-level executive, results-oriented, highly collaborative, driven performer, team player, strong work ethic, operates well under pressure, disciplined approach. They're clichés. Only use this language if that's what a position is requesting. But use it sparingly.

Here are a couple of examples of good, solid summaries. You don't have to be a brilliant writer to get your message across. You just need to be clear on what you want to say and know why it's there.

Fred: Real Estate Generalist

Fred has substantial experience in the real estate industry. He's worked in virtually every function as an investment professional on a wide range of projects, often involving complex structuring, many moving parts, and expert negotiation. The goal was to pack a punch in a brief statement so that his readers would not be burdened by having to process too much information. He knew that they would not welcome a long message.

Real Estate Investment Professional: Acquisitions, Direct Investment, Asset Management, and Finance

Originate, structure, execute, and manage complex real estate transactions globally, including large-scale and project-specific joint ventures with REIT's, Fortune 500 corporations, and private operating partners. Private equity, investment banking, and operating company experience as both a provider and end user of capital across the full spectrum of risk, from equity through mezzanine finance to senior debt.

Chris: Trader

Chris was a trader working for a large commercial bank. He had just been awarded the CFA designation and had passed each of the three levels on the first try. He was committed to using this newly acquired credential in making a move to the buy-side. He wanted initially to work as a trader and then transition to a portfolio management role. His summary statement was intended to capture his key areas of expertise, essentially exposure to a wide range of products, and to also convey his sincerity and commitment to pursuing this goal. He knew the competition would be intense. That's why he emphasizes the following information to differentiate himself: the combination of CFA and MBA, an analytical approach to trading, knowledge of numerous products, and a few personal characteristics that will make him stand out. Most important, it's short!

TRADING/INVESTMENT ANALYSIS/ PORTFOLIO MANAGEMENT:

CFA/MBA with substantial experience in analyzing, positioning, and executing trades across a variety of fixed income products, including investment grade corporate bonds, high yield, distressed, and emerging markets. Qualifications: Successful track record, reputation for integrity, and deep product knowledge.

Sarah: Back-Office Operations and Infrastructure

Sarah spent almost 20 years in back-office operations for a large global investment bank. She rotated through numerous assignments in three core areas: securities processing, technology, and compliance. Her goal was to work for a smaller institution in a more senior operations role, preferably an overseas bank with a limited presence in the United States and possibly intent on expansion. Her summary statement is intended to convey versatility and value. She's the operations equivalent of "one-stop shopping."

SENIOR PROJECT MANAGER—GLOBAL FINANCIAL SERVICES
• OPERATIONS • TECHNOLOGY • COMPLIANCE

Manage firm-wide projects and initiatives focused on quality, service, productivity, and cost containment. Point-person for key vendor relationships to maximize service delivery, standardize processes and costs, and implement important controls. Hands-on management style and deep knowledge base in core functional areas, including:

- **International Securities Settlements;** Managed area through dramatic growth and international migration.
- **Technology Network Management & Information;** Start-up of new departments with a focus on service providers.
- **Asset Management Compliance;** Streamlined procedures and contributed to significant growth.

On-going leadership responsibilities for acquisition of global services; regularly selected for numerous internal start-ups and turnaround situations.

Jane: Ex-Wall Street Managing Director Turned Not-for-Profit Executive

I've thrown this summary into the mix for those of you who may be looking for a more dramatic change. Jane was done with Wall Street. She made all the money she needed, and she was ready now to pursue an emerging passion. That's the point of this summary. It's not selling her knowledge of a financial product or service. Her goal was to convey her commitment to this new direction and to show that she was making all the right decisions to support this transition. It also offers a seal of approval; that important people and institutions now viewed her as having substance and credibility.

SUMMARY:

Ex-Wall Street executive deeply committed to making the world a better place. Skilled and experienced in starting up and building organizations through innovation, collaboration, respect, and passion. Wharton MBA. Member, Women's Leadership Board for the Kennedy School of Government at Harvard University.

Sandy: Hedge Fund Trader and Manager

Sandy is a man of few words. The language he uses is straightforward and intended to describe with some precision what he brings to a hedge fund. He's a trader and a hedge fund builder, and he has depth in all operational functions. It's also clear that he's good at what he does. He says that in a single word: profitably. He also makes it known that he has a terrific track record. This is a little self-promotion, but that's what his reader wants to see: He's smart, he makes a lot of money, and he knows how to build an organization from the ground up. He better be ready to defend his claims. Why include the CPA? To show that he has an appreciation for order, rules, and organization.

SUMMARY:

Hedge Fund specialist skilled in Portfolio Management, U.S. and International Trading, Strategy, Sales, Operations, and Risk Management. Expert in starting up, growing, and managing investment-based initiatives profitably. Outstanding track record developing hedge funds, broker dealer businesses, and strategic trading methodologies. Analytical, strategic, resourceful, motivated, focused, and results-oriented. Began career as CPA.

Rodney: Recent Graduate

Rodney was in the process of completing one of the top masters programs in Real Estate. Except for being a partner in a small retail establishment prior to graduate school, he had no formal work experience in the industry. He was only 23, and he was competing against more seasoned candidates for entry-level positions. Rather than focus on his life before school, his summary needed to present a resource whose potential had not yet been tapped. That's why a high GPA, strong skills in analysis, research, and financial modeling, and the ability to use industry-specific technology were critical. It was also important to show Rodney's ongoing commitment to continuing education to strengthen his skills as an analyst—that is, preparing for level 2 of the CFA exam.

Associate: Real Estate Investment Analysis

Recent NYU-MS graduate in Real Estate Finance and Investments (3.9 GPA) with strong skills and background in the analysis of diverse real estate opportunities. Longstanding interest and experience in the real estate industry both as an investor and retailer. Have reviewed a wide range of transactions using advanced financial modeling, rigorous research, and cash flow analysis. Proficiency using Excel, Argus; Level II Candidate in the CFA Program.

Dan: Technology

Dan was working for a large consulting firm, and after several years, he was ready to move to the client side. His clients were global investment banking firms, and he traveled extensively for assignments. Although he loved the work, he was tired of living out of a suitcase for many months at a time. The theme of his summary: to demonstrate his potential to add value immediately, to convey his interest in a more strategic technology role, and to show his understanding of issues and challenges facing these firms.

Capital Markets IT Professional

Senior technology professional and strategist skilled in partnering with line business management to deliver business change through Information Technology. Deep knowledge of global capital markets products, processes, and services. Consistently achieve ambitious business goals in fast-paced, global organizations by bridging the IT/business gap and applying a diversified blend of technologies. Personal strengths include an end-to-end solution focus, an ability to operate successfully in complex and multi-cultural environments, and a unique talent for motivating high-performing teams to go above and beyond. Areas of expertise include:

- Enterprise Reference Data Management
- Global Asset Management Accounting
- Global Project Management
- Offshore Development
- Implementation Methodology

Career Change Resumes: Jim and Andre

Jim was a proprietary trader for almost 20 years. He worked for several institutions and acquired substantial experience across multiple products and all maturities. He was introduced to me shortly after his firm advised him that his position was being eliminated. They offered him a couple of months' notice and the opportunity to keep his seat on the desk while looking for a job. There should be no debate over the relative benefits of looking for a job while you appear to be working. It's always better.

Despite some anger over being separated involuntarily, Jim intended to use the time productively. He began his job search in a systematic and organized approach. First, he and I focused our attention on establishing targets; then we worked together to prepare his resume. Next, we developed his story to position the transition, and at that point, he was ready to network. In truth, Jim could have begun networking immediately. He just needed to feel absolutely secure in his target before he graduated to the next level and went "prime-time." Although he was not entirely certain about the next steps, he did know that being a trader was no longer a desirable option.

Through various assessment exercises, Jim identified a single target that he was most excited to pursue: operational risk management. Networking was intended as an exploratory process. He was eager to get started and began work on his resume. The first document he produced was a standard issue chronological resume...Jim's career as a trader. It was about two pages in length, and it did absolutely nothing to position him for a career change.

If your goal is to make a career change, that theme must be reflected in your resume. As a career changer, I encouraged Jim to replace the word "Summary" at the very top of his resume with the words "Professional Objective and Background." It sounded solid, determined, and unequivocally clear as to his intentions. That's also the standard profile of the risk management professional reading his resume. It's not a bad idea to survey your readers—in this case, risk managers—to identify key themes and characteristics that you and they share in common. Notice also how Jim demonstrates that risk management is a consistent theme throughout his career. Jim doesn't ignore the fact that he was a trader. He just uses his role and former career as the reason to explain how he came to be an expert in risk management. Each of the bullet points in his summary drives this message home.

Notice that the "Professional Experience" section only briefly describes each of his roles. Why belabor the obvious? He was a trader whose trading performance was no longer as important as the lessons he learned on the job. Again, the language emphasizes risk management techniques, increasing knowledge as a subject matter expert, special projects to demonstrate his commitment to this function, and his recognition of its importance.

Jim's Resume

JIM   Cell: xxx-xxx-xxxx

Street Address   Home: xxx-xxx-xxxx

City, State Zip   Email: xxxxxxx@xxx.com

PROFESSIONAL OBJECTIVE & BACKGROUND:

Operational Risk Management/Strategy/Advisory

Particular emphasis on operational risk measures; best practices in evaluating quantitative and qualitative risk issues; new product approval; regulatory liaison, i.e. self-compliance procedures; and optimizing operational processes using technology. Highlights include:

- *Substantial experience applying quantitative, qualitative, and regulatory expertise in a variety of Capital Markets roles: as a trader, market maker, risk manager, and operations/accounting officer.*
- *On-going role interfacing with technology to streamline front-office systems. Excellent knowledge of front-office real-time risk management solutions.*
- *Deep understanding of the risk management process.*
- *[NAME OF SCHOOL] MBA, completed night program in three years.*

PROFESSIONAL EXPERIENCE

[NAME OF INSTITUTION]; SVP (XXXX–Present)

- Proprietary Trader and Risk Manager of [FILL IN THE CATEGORY OF PRODUCTS] across all maturity sectors. Experienced in trading [NAMES OF THE VARIOUS PRODUCTS]. Responsible for gathering and distributing market intelligence on a timely basis. Assisted in the testing and implementation of front-end trading systems.

[NAME OF INSTITUTION]; Vice President (DATES)

- Market Maker and Proprietary Trader of [PRODUCT NAME(S)] within the five- to ten-year sector of the curve. Responsible for the development of trade ideas and analysis of swap opportunities for both propriety and customer accounts throughout the yield curve. Market maker across the curve providing seamless execution for institutional clients. Designated Trader Liaison for testing and implementing front-end trading systems.

[NAME OF INSTITUTION]; MD (DATES)

- Responsible for managing and executing the liabilities of the portfolio. Analyzed and managed the risks within all sectors of the [PRODUCT CATEGORY] yield curve to further enhance the performance of the portfolio. Traded all Repurchase Agreements to minimize the borrowing cost associated with the liabilities.

[NAME OF INSTITUTION]; MD (DATES)

- Market Maker, Proprietary Trader and Risk Manager of [PRODUCT CATEGORY] within the two- to ten-year sector. Market insight, idea generation, and timely execution supported risk management in various departments. Aggressive market making in all sectors, other than assigned, maintaining customer relationships. Assisted in the analysis and selection of technology systems for the [NAME OF PRODUCT] Department.

[NAME OF INSTITUTION]; VP, Sr Trader (DATES)

- Propriety Trader and Market Maker for all [NAME OF PRODUCT], zero through five years. Experienced Institutional and Proprietary Trader of [NAME OF SECOND PRODUCT] within five-year maturities.

[NAME OF INSTITUTION]; (DATES)

- Responsible for staffing, accounting, and P&L of the Repurchase Agreements for Fixed Income.

> **EDUCATION**
>
> **[GRADUATE SCHOOL] (DATES),** MBA
>
> **[UNDERGRADUATE SCHOOL] (DATES),** BBA
>
> **Registrations:** NASD—Series 7 and Series 63

Andre's Resume

You may recall Andre from the chapter on assessment. He was the institutional salesperson who made the move to an analyst position on the buy-side. Like Jim, Andre began his career in an accounting role and then eventually made the move to trading. After a couple of years, he shifted again to institutional sales. Every job was a variation on the same theme: analyzing and positioning complex trades and developing trading strategies. That's the message that Andre needed to convey on his resume.

The summary header explains what he wants, and the three bullets that follow outline his qualifications. The first bullet shows the breadth and depth of his experience and the clients he's worked with. The second bullet explains the types of complex trades he's executed. The third bullet emphasizes his academic background and his ability to apply his skills immediately.

The body of Andre's resume is divided into two sections: the last several years in institutional sales at three firms and his life before in trading. Notice how each header emphasizes his subject matter expertise. Even the educational entries are focused on neutralizing his roles in sales in large part due to the perception, whether true or false, that sales may be less rigorous intellectually than analysis. Andre does this by using language to demonstrate how smart he is: his rank in a very large and competitive college, the fact that he graduated with distinction from a top business school, and the CFA designation.

ANDRE, CFA   xxx xxx-xxxx (Home), xxx xxx-xxxx (Mobile)

Street Address, City, State Zip   E-Mail: xxxxxxx@xxx.com

Objective & Background:
Analysis/Trading of Distressed Debt for Hedge
Fund/Prop Desk

- Extensive experience in analyzing, structuring, and executing trades with hedge funds across corporate bonds, structured products, emerging markets, and rates.
- Trading strategies executed include capital structure trades, directional trades, basis trades, convexity trades, index trades, and structured credit trades.
- Strong fundamental analysis including financial modeling/presenting to credit committee, valuation of investments, and bankruptcy law. CFA, MBA, CPA.

CREDIT DERIVATIVES/BOND SALES TO HEDGE   **xxxx–Present**
FUNDS

[NAME OF 1st INSTITUTION], **SVP, Credit Sales**   xxxx–Present

[NAME OF 2nd INSTITUTION], **VP, Credit Sales**   xxxx–xxxx

[NAME OF 3rd INSTITUTION], **VP, EM Sales**   xxxx–xxxx

- At [1st INSTITUTION], sell trade ideas in corporate bonds, credit default swaps, swaptions, tranches, cdos, recovery rates, and indices to hedge funds producing $— mm annualized.
- At [2nd INSITUTION], grew hedge fund clients in credit derivatives from $— to $—. Hired and managed team of x. Own production exceeded $— million in xxxx and xxxx. #1 salesperson xxxx to xxxx. Presented at client conferences and for internal education.
- At [3rd INSTITUTION], sold EM bonds (bradies, sovereign, corporates) and local currencies (GKOs, Zloty, NDFs in Latin America) to hedge funds and money managers. #1 salesperson within two years of starting.

TRADING/RESEARCH/ANALYSIS

[NAME OF 4th INSTITUTION], City, State   (Overall Dates)

Head Trader, Treasury Division (DATES)

- Top-producing trader [YEARS], managing the bank's interest rate risk using money market instruments, futures, swaps, and options. Managed team of x traders.
- Grew treasury division's profits from $— million in [YEAR] to $— million in [YEAR], making the division the largest profit center at the bank in [YEAR].

Research Associate, Capital Markets (DATES)

- Performed rigorous research on topics such as lease-backed securities and ARMs.
- Completed nine-month credit/corporate finance training program. Analyzed and presented various credits to the bank's Credit Committee.

[NAME OF GRADUATE SCHOOL], Location

MBA—Finance, Graduation Date. Graduated with Distinction—top 5%.

Between [YEARS], led audit teams at **[NAME OF BIG 4 FIRM]** for clients in the following industries: ————, ———, ————, and ————.

[NAME OF UNDERGRADUATE SCHOOL], Location

BA in [Major], Graduation Date. Ranked #x out of xxxx

John: Job Hopper and Career Changer

John contacted me after reading an article in *Money Magazine* in which I was featured. As one of four experts on a career panel—a recruiter, a financial advisor, an image consultant, and me—we were asked to work with three individuals in various stages of job search. Like the three clients in the article, John felt that he had hit a brick wall. He was a foreign exchange trader with a long career marked by great success early on, followed by a series of rapid moves. He started out as an assistant on a trading desk and was promoted quickly. Then the moves began. Some were due to restructurings, one or two to a political melt-down, and two through recruiters presenting packages that he couldn't ignore.

It was a complicated story to tell in person...to tell it on paper was even more challenging. He had worked for six banks, and some of the assignments were short term. Most of the moves had been made for all the right reasons at the time. Viewed in hindsight and collectively, his career history was a real mess. Our goal was to create a resume that didn't look like a list of one job after another. We were going to demonstrate a sense of purpose, and offer major value. The point was to get the reader to pay attention and not eliminate John from consideration before an in-person meeting. It was also to position John for a career change. He felt like he had outgrown the trading desk and wanted to move to the client side in a corporate treasury position. John was a great and passionate trader and smart about the business, too—but he was ready to pursue a new direction. He and I didn't want the resume to be an unnecessary barrier and have him eliminated before a first conversation.

I wasn't expecting the resume to perform magic. John's resume and history would always be a problem; we just wanted it to be less of a problem. The goal was to get him in front of as many people as possible. Because he was making a career change, I also knew that traditional job search via recruiters and job postings was not the answer either. He would need to tap into a longstanding network on the corporate side. I knew that the reader of his resume would benefit from advance warning as to his intentions. That's why John's resume clearly and precisely explains from the top of his summary statement what he wants. The summary also outlines his qualifications that would be attractive to a corporate position and highlights several of the global organizations he's worked for. That's meant to show that he speaks "corporate."

The "Career Highlights" section is brief. It's a listing of a few key qualifications and achievements; then they're followed by a list of the banks where he worked. It's simple, straightforward, and brief, and there are no distractions. The real focus is the summary statement.

JOHN

Street

City, State Zip

Cell: xxx xxx-xxxx; E-mail: xxxxxxx@xxx.com

PROFILE AND OBJECTIVE:

Treasury Position in Exposure/Risk Management

<u>Structure risk management strategies</u> for corporate clients to minimize foreign exchange risk and maximize profit potential in my role as a trader. Work closely and productively with the sales team. Have in-depth knowledge of spot and forward trading, options, and interest rates. I'm frequently recognized by senior management for: <u>maintaining the highest standards, operating well under pressure and in crisis, and achieving a consistently outstanding track record</u>.

Recruited to work for the following global institutions:

- A   • B   • C   • D   • E

CAREER HIGHLIGHTS

- Senior Trader on Institution C's European desk. Highest producer in [YEAR].
- Consolidated and expanded Institution D's foreign exchange operation for Asia Pacific, based in [LOCATION].
- Managed Institution D's Tokyo foreign exchange unit of xx traders and also traded the —- spot and forward portfolios.
- Direct liaison for Institution A's largest and most important customer in [LOCATION].
- Recruited to increase Institution E's exposure to Asia Pacific currencies. Moved on to trade [COUNTRY] and [COUNTRY] dollars, establishing the bank as a leading market maker.

INSTITUTION A
Vice President, Foreign Exchange—Location
INSTITUTION B
Director, Foreign Exchange—Location
INSTITUTION C
Vice President, Foreign Exchange—Location
INSTITUTION D
Manager, Foreign Exchange Trading—Location
Manager, Foreign Exchange Trading—Different Location
Senior Dealer—Different Location
INSTITUTION E
Foreign Exchange Dealer—Location
INSTITUTION F
Foreign Exchange Dealer—Location

EDUCATION

NAME OF UNIVERSITY, Location (city and state if U.S. *or* city and country if overseas)

Major: xxxxx, Graduation Date

Honors/Awards/Scholarships: xxxxxxxxxxx; Activities: Sports, Clubs, and so on

Ken: Investment Banker

Ken's resume is a combination of several client resumes. The resume mixes and matches aspects of three different clients, each with the same goal—to work in either private equity or investment banking—and many of the same personal and professional characteristics. It's a generic format that works for standard issue investment bankers who are pursuing highly competitive positions. It's the post-MBA resume, a variation on the model used by many business schools. This more traditional resume is in no way a less effective approach. In fact, it's just the opposite. If your audience has well-established expectations for a familiar format, work in that format. It's always better to give them what they want but to do so in a way that gets them to pay attention for the right reasons.

In this type of resume, address the basics: where, when, and how well. You don't need to add much more information than that—the padding buys you virtually no measurable advantage. In this format, the content makes a difference, not the presentation. The goal is to have the interviewer's attention focused around you as a candidate and the value you have the potential to bring. Your resume should not raise any unnecessary questions. If there *are* a couple of detours that require explanation, then you do so using this format.

This resume breaks just about every rule, as follows:

- There's no summary statement. Why bother?
- The dates are listed on the left. Readers have a driving need to know when and for how long...they're mathematicians.
- There's not much in the way of commentary. The skills are fairly generic. It's your performance that should be front and center.
- It's not seamless; it's intended to show life primarily after business school with a minimum amount of attention devoted to life before.
- Much of the language is about success: winning, academic excellence, athletic accomplishments, credentials, and language proficiencies.

KEN   Cell: xxx xxx-xxxx; E-mail: xxxxxxx@xxx.com

Street; City, State Zip

EXPERIENCE

(DATE)   **GLOBAL INVESTMENT BANK (GIB)**

VP, Media, Telecom & Entertainment (DATES)

Associate, Media, Telecom & Entertainment (DATES)

- Managed day-to-day relationships and project execution for clients in the media and telecom sectors; managed a team of top associates in performing strategic and financial analyses to help companies grow, fund corporate initiatives, and execute strategic transactions.

- Oversaw various valuation analyses, developed investment theses, prepared positioning and marketing materials, managed day-to-day management team relationship and execution of COMPANY A's acquisition of a 25% stake in COMPANY B.

- Led and worked with client company operations and senior management during due diligence, prepared senior executives for negotiations, worked with joint team (Client, Legal, GIB) to structure transaction, and presented at Board meeting while representing COMPANY C in acquiring COMPANY D.

- Primary relationship contact for CFO of publicly traded, branded apparel manufacturer; developed, with client and GIB team, acquisition strategy and preparation for dialogues with potential combination partners.

- Led marketing effort to build business with publicly traded media company with over $1 billion market capitalization by developing relationship with business development executives.

(SUMMER DATE)	**PRIVATE EQUITY FIRM**

- Assisted management of portfolio company to successfully raise $30 million in second-round financing.
- Developed market strategy, product positioning, and financial model for Board of Directors review.

(DATES)	**GLOBAL CONSULTING FIRM**

Senior Consultant, Corporate Finance Group

- Performed financial and strategic analysis to evaluate capital markets alternatives for real estate companies.

Selected Advisory Assignments:

- Private real estate company's $50 million equity private placement for its first real estate fund.
- Industrial property company's sale of 825,000 square feet of holdings and 100 acres of developable land.

EDUCATION

(YEARS)	**GRADUATE SCHOOL OF BUSINESS**

MBA (Graduation Date)

- President, Finance Club

(YEARS)	**UNDERGRADUATE UNIVERSITY**

BA, History with Honors & Distinction (Graduation Date)

- Phi Beta Kappa; Varsity Track

ADDITIONAL

- Fluent Spanish, proficient Russian; Series 7 certified
- Training for NYC Marathon; scuba diving; golf; adventure travel
- Detailed list of transactions attached

Roger: Hedge Fund Manager and Founder

Here's another example of a resume that requires no introduction. Roger started and managed two hedge funds. His goal is to either work for an established hedge fund as a portfolio manager or co-found another fund. A summary statement would be pointless. His reader doesn't need that information. It should be obvious from Roger's resume what he wants and why. That means providing content on the resume that will distinguish Roger from other candidates, as follows:

- Performance information to demonstrate his track record and success.
- Areas of investment focus and product specialization that showcase him as a subject matter expert.
- Like Ken, the investment banker whose resume precedes this one, a history of success and accomplishment both professionally and academically.
- Most important, being mindful that his reader will not respond well to a long story.

ROGER, CFA

Street, Apartment; City, State Zip

Cell: xxx xxx-xxxx; E-Mail: xxxxxxx@xxx.com

HEDGE FUND A, Location

Principal and Co-Founder (DATES)

- Co-founded multi-strategy credit hedge fund that invested in high-yield debt, equities, distressed debt, and capital structure arbitrage.
- Marketed the fund to potential investors and managed the fund's relationships with investors.
- Grew assets from $x million to $xxx million.
- Generated average annualized return of x %.

HEDGE FUND B, Location
Principal and Co-Founder (DATES)

- Co-founded multi-strategy hedge fund using investment strategy similar to Hedge Fund A.
- Grew assets under management from $xx million to $xxx million.
- Generated average annualized return of x %.

INVESTMENT MANAGEMENT FIRM, Location
Senior Vice President (DATES)

- Managed a proprietary trading account.
- Senior analyst covering distressed/bankrupt companies.

GLOBAL INVESTMENT BANK, Location
Vice President, Corporate Bond Research (DATES)

- Senior analyst covering high-yield and distressed companies in the following sectors: ———, ———, ———, ———, ———, and ———.
- Recommended successful proprietary trading ideas for the trading desks.
- Published targeted monthly research report for [#] buy-side clients and [#] corporate customers in addition to periodic reports.
- Marketed [#] lead-managed high-yield transactions totaling over $x billion.

PENSION FUND MANAGER, Location
Associate, Private Placement Division (DATES)

- Analyzed credit quality for $x hundred million in securities purchases. Negotiated structure/covenant packages and managed legal due diligence.

FORTUNE 500 COMPANY, Location
Mortgage-Backed Securities Analyst and Trader (DATES)
Training Program (DATES)

EDUCATION

GRADUATE SCHOOL OF BUSINESS, Location

MBA with concentration in ——— (DATE); Honors and Awards: ————; Teaching Assistant, Finance Dept.

<u>Summer Associate</u>, Global Financial Institution

UNDERGRADUATE SCHOOL, Location

BA in ——— (DATE); Honors and Awards

Activities (Clubs and Athletics): ———-, ————-, ———,

————.

<u>Summer Internships:</u>

- ————- (YEAR)
- ————- (YEAR)

The Hybrid Resume

I've been coaching Wall Street clients for a long time. I've reviewed and helped prepare thousands of resumes. The Hybrid is a format I had never seen before so, of course, I'll take credit for introducing it. Sure, it probably exists elsewhere, but it did emerge out of a conversation with a client whose background on paper needed to be simplified visually. It's also been used with great success by many of my other clients. That means it has great potential to work for you, too. It felt like an obvious solution for a particular kind of client: a senior executive with numerous accomplishments and a long story to tell, a project manager with multiple assignments over an extended period of time, or a person who's had nine lives professionally.

The Hybrid is a resume with two parts. The first page is a condensed version of your resume. It's only one page, not more or less, with plenty of white space. It's all there with only a highlight or two for each job that's included. It begins with a summary that captures the essential message you want the reader to take away: what you're positioned for, what qualifies you, and why. It might even suggest how the reader stands to benefit. The summary ties it all together. If you're clear on what you want to do and your qualifications match what your reader is looking for, then you've got a love connection. This first page is the hook. Give them a teaser, get them excited, and know that they'll want more if you touch on relevant themes and challenges that may be important to them. If the reader likes what is presented on the first page, he or she will be hungry for additional detail. That's the goal.

The format tends to work best for clients who have a lot to say. If that's the case, you can't and shouldn't throw your reader into the deep end of the pool immediately. Too much information too soon will overwhelm. This is not a debate. Your resume will not get the time and attention it deserves.

The following resume was prepared by a fellow who spent almost 25 years at the same investment bank. He worked in a variety of departments and roles primarily in back- and middle-office positions. Notice how the first page is constructed. He begins with a powerful and informative summary statement. The goal: to demonstrate his versatility, as well as the depth and breadth of his experience and knowledge. Because he's positioning the resume for hedge funds, that's where most of his attention is focused. His two most recent assignments at hedge funds convey his value, whereas his 25 prior years at the global investment bank establish his credibility.

Page two provides detail and highlights on his various roles at some of the firms. There was no need to include every assignment; just those that were more important or supported his search for a hedge fund position. That's why he omitted the commodities firm. It was a direction he no longer had an interest in pursuing. Regarding the global investment bank, he could have provided a lot more of his history there—and for some of you, that would make sense—but he knew that his particular reader would appreciate only information that could be quickly digested and demonstrate immediate benefit.

NAME

Street

City, State Zip

(M): xxx xxx-xxxx; E-Mail: xxxxxxx@xxx.com

Specialist in Back-Office & Middle-Office Operations:

In-depth buy- and sell-side experience across key functions: <u>Accounting</u>, <u>Operations</u>, <u>Technology</u>, <u>Compliance</u>, <u>Legal</u>, <u>and Credit</u>. Support senior management through rigorous evaluation of processes and financial operations to improve decision making. Identify areas for the business to act "smarter," reduce operating expenses, and consistently generate revenue. Top performer at (GLOBAL INVESTMENT BANK); currently specialize in <u>hedge fund operations and administration</u>.

PROFESSIONAL EXPERIENCE

HEDGE FUND A, City, State (Dates)

VP/Assistant Treasurer

- Recruited by CFO to analyze hedge fund operations for opportunities to improve efficiencies, reduce costs, and improve relationships with prime brokers. Following rapid expansion of the funds, management was concerned about being overcharged. Also established and managed a securities lending profit center for security borrows, lending longs, and dividend yield enhancement. Added over $xxx million to the bottom line within three years.

HEDGE FUND B, City, State (Dates)

VP, Operations

- Leadership responsibility for day-to-day operations, processes, and controls for diversified hedge fund manager. Chief of staff and right hand to the COO. Involved in a wide range of special projects including: systems implementation, procedures documentation, and disaster recovery.

GLOBAL COMMODITIES FIRM, City, State (Dates)

- Operations Consultant, start-up Structured Products Group

GLOBAL INVESTMENT BANK, City, State (Dates)

VP/Administrator

VP/Manager

Manager, Back-Office Operations

- Began career in (DEPARTMENT A) with responsibility for (FUNCTION) and then promoted to manager of (PRODUCT) operations. Moved to trading desk as liaison between trading and the rest of the firm. Promoted to Chief Administrator for (DEPARTMENT B).

PUBLIC ACCOUNTING FIRM, Certified Public Accountants (Dates)

Auditor

EDUCATION

BS in Accounting, Date; **UNIVERSITY**, City, State

Honors: —————, —————. Member, Accounting Society

CPA, Awarded (YEAR)

Name   **Page Two**

E-Mail: xxxxxxx@xxx.com; (M): xxx xxx-xxxx

DETAILED CAREER HIGHLIGHTS

HEDGE FUND A, City, State (Dates)

VP/Assistant Treasurer

- Analyzed all (PRODUCT) and corrected over $xx in mischarges.
- Drove the implementation of (PROCESS) to the firm, earning in excess of $xx million over the last two years.
- Designed comprehensive reports to monitor (PROCESS) across prime brokers to better position HEDGE FUND A

to get the best rates and to support movement between prime brokers to take advantage of these rates.

- Sourced hard to borrow securities for the trade execution desk.

- Implemented a methodology to identify stock-lending opportunities for long positions that generated revenue of $xx million.

- Automated the manual reconciliation of futures positions. Reduced daily processing time, eliminated human error, and increased scalability of the business.

- Aggressively negotiated financing rates with prime brokers for cash borrow/lend rates, margin levels, futures execution rates, custody fees, etc.

- Leveraged prime brokerage relationships to improve service and get committed facilities in place.

- Recommended to senior management to draw down all allowable cash under committed facilities to prevent liquidity concerns and for investment.

HEDGE FUND B, City, State (Dates)

VP, Operations

- Opened communication channels with prime brokers to resolve outstanding operational issues, including new process to review prime broker trade settlement.

- Managed team that provided service to the Trading Desk. Earned the reputation for getting things done. For example, standardized a Stock Borrow Report among numerous prime brokers.

- Re-engineered operational processes and workflows including confirmations, executing brokers, trade break reconciliations, settlement fails, and various control gaps.

- Managed on-time rollout of (SYSTEM), which eliminated duplicate processing and produced greater efficiencies and control in the day-to-day flow.

- Initiated plans for Disaster Recovery, including leased space with desks and hardware for business continuity.

- Established metrics reporting methodology for the preparation of senior management reports.
- Oversaw daily cash receipts and disbursements for over xxx bank accounts.

GLOBAL INVESTMENT BANK, City, State (Dates)
VP/Administrator
VP/Manager
Manager, Back-Office Operations

- Administrator for xxx person (DEPARTMENT) and point person for Division administrative issues, interface between traders and controllers.
- Responsible for all administrative and operations functions on the (PRODUCT) Desk. Liaison between the Desk and downstream support groups (operations, controllers, credit, legal) including coordination for new product implementation and initiating controls. Resident authority on (SUBJECT).
- Discovered differential opportunities that added $x million profit to the Desk. Oversaw (FUNCTION) with value up to $xxx million each.
- Established and maintained successful central bank relationships, personally generating over $xxx for the GLOBAL INVESTMENT BANK. Responsible for the Bank's operational relationship with (ORGANIZATION).
- Managed operations staff of xx through large variations of daily business activity with significant exposures. Set up and maintained new procedures continually as the business grew and changed.
- Coordinated the Desk's orders; signed off on select confirms; prepared monthly accruals for expenses such as brokerage and freight; and reviewed the daily business to catch and correct errors; general troubleshooting.
- Maintained trading positions throughout the day. Monitored exchange limits and arranged for hedge exemptions. Reviewed transactions with brokers/trading counterparties.

The Speed Resume

The Speed Resume shouldn't take you more than an hour or two to prepare. It's not intended to replace your real resume. That will take time, memory, and real work to create. This is a quick fix. It's just an approach, not a resume format.

Say you find yourself in the following situation. You've been asked to submit a resume ASAP. You don't have one yet or the one you have is not appropriate for the opportunity that's been presented to you. You're in a bind, and you need to move fast. There's a deadline, some urgency to the request. Better to submit something—anything, for that matter—than to risk losing out or being overlooked. You can always present a modified and enhanced version later on after you've had the time to create a document that makes you proud. In the meantime, just get something in. It's easy to explain the second revised version at the right time: *I was eager to get a resume to you, and I rushed to pull one together. Here's an updated version, which I feel better represents my background and accomplishments. It also, I feel, explains why I'm so excited about this opportunity.*

Here are the steps. Follow them, and you'll have a resume that's good enough for the time being. Getting it perfect will take some time:

1. List all of the organizations you've worked for in reverse chronological order...most recent first. Within each company, do the same for the various jobs you've held.

2. For each job, list your responsibilities.

3. For each job, describe a homerun or two...an accomplishment that comes easily to mind. What was the issue or challenge? What did you do to address the issue? What was the outcome?

4. Now set this work aside. If you have a job description, great. Find one or two additional similar jobs online through a job posting board. Highlight relevant language that's used to describe the role, its key responsibilities, and qualifications in an ideal candidate.

5. Take this language and make sure you use it in providing the details for each of your past jobs. Whoever is reading the resume—even if it's being scanned by a machine—will need to see that the language you use to describe yourself is the language of the job you're applying for. It's just another step to help you make it past the gatekeeper.

6. Decide if a summary statement is needed to explain why your background and qualifications are appropriate. It may not be. If what you've done is what you want to do *and* what they're looking for in an ideal candidate, then skip it! If not, you can build a summary quickly. Again, just use the language that's been presented in the job description and other postings. Also see the "The Summary Statement" section in this chapter for examples. Please feel free to plagiarize!

7. Decide how far back you want and need to go. If the description is explicit in stating the number of years of experience desired, say 10 to 15, then going back for 25 years may be unnecessary or potentially damaging.

8. Proof the resume for typos and grammatical errors.

Remember, the Speed Resume is just a temporary substitute. It may be great—a 30-minute work of wonder—and I hope that's the case. But chances are, it will require some tweaking. You may have overlooked essential information whose absence diminishes you as a candidate. Your reader may have a short attention span, but you can't afford that yourself. That's unacceptable if you've made a commitment to successfully navigating job search.

6

Networking: Just Do It, Please

A *network* describes the system and framework by which information is communicated. It happens through a series of nodes or connection points that are programmed to recognize, process, and forward important information to other nodes. Networks also interconnect with other networks and with sub-networks to form a complex Web or system of pathways...the ultimate goal to transmit data. What possible relevance does it have for you, your career, and job search...unless you're looking for a job in technology? It has everything to do with your job search and how you manage your career. In tough job markets and in better ones, too, job search requires networking, and networking relies heavily on understanding and mobilizing the various technologies at your disposal. Networks replay and circulate the key news about you and your brand.

When you're in job search, you want your network to expand exponentially—online, offline, and everywhere. Networking is much more than meeting people and collecting contact information. Open networks, with many weak ties (referrals and social connections) as well as strong ties (friends, family, and close work associates), are more likely to introduce ideas and opportunities than closed networks with few external relationships. This describes the model network for our current economy and job market in 2010 and beyond.

Effective networking connects your strong ties to a wider network of weak ties with individuals connected to other social worlds. It is better for your success to have connections to a variety of networks rather than many connections within a single network (such as friends at your old job).

In job search, your goal is to identify every resource to expand your reach. If this sounds vaguely familiar, it should. Think LinkedIn or Facebook—two examples of technology-based social networking tools. When we network, we are gathering and sharing information with the specific goal of establishing and nurturing productive relationships to support our businesses, careers, and friendships.

In the current and future job market, if you don't network, you don't job search, and in all likelihood, you won't meet your goal. Managing a dynamic job search and an equally dynamic career means taking a more aggressive approach to how you manage and, yes, exploit relationships. You have no choice. There's too much riding on your willingness (or resistance) to jump in—even more important, to jump in and swim. From my experience, that's the difference between a reluctant client and one who's successful in search. Yes, it's having a strategy. It's also about committing yourself to reaching out and beyond and often into areas that may be unfamiliar and uncomfortable. For most of you, the easy part is figuring out who to network with. It's much harder to execute this strategy. Everyone has some networking baggage. Networking taps into our innate fear of the unfamiliar, of the power of new relationships to judge us, change us, and affect us. This fear is part of our "old brain" that has us biologically wired to be cautious with unknown competitors in our environment. But this is no different than many such fears of being exposed by the unknown. Drawing on our judgment and reason, we do the unfamiliar. By overcoming this instinctive fear, we gain power, confidence, insights, and the security of having a wider network.

As examples go, here's one that may not elicit a lot of sympathy. It's about networking among the very rich and successful. One of my former clients, Steve, was the COO of a hedge fund. When the fund was wound down, he found himself in job search for the first time since college and almost 23 years since he had last been interviewed.

He was around 50 at the time and committed to continuing in his career. Mind you, he didn't have to—he wanted to. That was the strange contradiction. When I asked him about his network and the resources he could tap into to expand his universe of contacts, I got back an uncomfortable silence. Steve was a member of a yacht club in Connecticut and a bridge club in New York City. These were gold-mines. Both were made up of peers and decision makers at many of the firms that were desirable to Steve.

What was holding Steve back? It was the belief that his peers and friends would see him as less competent than he was, maybe even a failure. Despite the fact that the fund was dissolved at the right time in the market, it still left him feeling exposed and vulnerable: *If I were so great, how come no one is pursuing me?* That's because Steve didn't let anyone know. When he finally put the word out that he was available and wanting to work, he received considerable support, advice, and information. It was only a matter of time before he landed.

The Elements of Effective Networking

Before I offer you a strategy for networking, let's consider what it takes to be successful in job search—a mini review. How does job search happen? By actively using four techniques: responding to ads and postings, getting introduced by recruiters, writing direct and tar-geted letters—translate: primarily e-mail—and last, but not least, networking. It's not complicated. It's just a lot of work and an enor-mous amount of detail to manage. Networking is the job search equivalent of a routine visit to the dentist. You know it's good for you, you need to go, but you try to avoid the visit for as long as possible. It's the unexpected and unwelcome discovery that often keeps us on the fence when it comes to scheduling an appointment.

From my experience, the biggest challenges in networking, at least in the beginning, have to do with efficiency and logistics—who to network with, what to ask for, and how often. Remember, networking is not connecting with your closest friends and colleagues repeatedly. It's about building up your "weak ties." It's not unusual for Wall Street clients to tell me that they feel overwhelmed by the prospect of moving out of their circle. They've just never done it before, or if they have, it's often on behalf of the company they work for. The visibility and exposure leave many of them feeling vulnerable, and that's not a familiar emotion and experience. It shifts the balance of power. The implication is also that networking means you're either out of work or unhappy at work, and that's a sign of personal failure. Is this reasoning logical? Of course, it's not, but you and I don't always look at situations rationally.

Why network? The competition for available opportunities is getting more and more intense. Relying on traditional search strategies like recruiting firms and ads means that you will only be exposed to a small percentage of open jobs. More important, you won't hear about the jobs that are not publicized. It's also like giving someone else the keys to the car. You're no longer in the driver's seat. Networking is not really about job search. It's about establishing a community that is ever expanding and changing—a universe of professional colleagues who believe in you and support your career.

Of course, the ultimate goal is to get a job or to keep your job. You know that, and so do they. Networking is how you get there. You use networking tools to collect information, to establish career-long and sometimes life-long relationships, to get referrals, and to be remembered. People help people they know and like. Remember this point! People help people they like.

When Networking Backfires: Emily

When you go out into the world in your job search, please be careful that you don't take a lack of response personally. Most people you contact are busy, or they should be. All you have control over is how you present yourself—what you do and say and how you follow-up. It's up to them—whoever your audience may be—to respond. You can't force it or them. Your goal is give them a reason to be intrigued by you and to want to get to know you better.

Networking is just one tool you use to establish relationships. When do you cross the line from networker to stalker? Getting a meeting takes persistence, good humor, and patience. During the meeting, it should become clear what sort of information and support will be forthcoming. When you try to force more out of the conversation than you deserve or the interviewer is willing to share, you've got a problem. When you follow-up repeatedly after the meeting for more and more information, or to request favors, you've got an even bigger problem. That's stalking. Moderation is essential, and so is expressing gratitude for any shred of help that's been offered. Don't abuse the privilege.

Emily was referred to me by another career counselor. The two of them had reached an impasse in their work together. It wasn't an unfriendly divorce. Emily was eager to begin her search, and her counselor didn't have sufficient understanding as to Emily's professional direction and interests. She was an investment banker who wanted to make the transition to private equity. She had all the right stuff: a great pedigree, good schools, and top-tier investment banking experience.

I made the mistake of assuming that Emily was ready to network without first establishing the ground rules. Then I made an even bigger mistake—I introduced her to a former client of mine, Jack, who successfully made the move from investment banking to private equity a few years before. He was a terrific fellow and well-liked; she seemed knowledgeable and focused. From my perspective, it was a perfect match—the equivalent of a networking love connection. It wasn't. In fact, it was a disaster.

Unfortunately, this is a great example of how good intentions without good planning and equally good judgment don't necessarily accomplish their goal. It's also a lesson you can learn at my expense. I assumed that Emily understood what networking was intended to accomplish, especially at this early stage of her job search. The meeting should have served as a forum for gathering information: about private equity as an industry, how to transition, firms to get to know, key players. An opportunity to ask the question: If you were me, how would you make the move? I thought that Emily realized that Jack had made himself available as both a professional courtesy and as a favor to me. Instead, she took advantage of the situation.

Emily approached her meeting with Jack as an entitlement rather than a gift. She viewed Jack as a resource and lead generator and as a source for names. Without so much as explaining why she wanted to make the move or what qualified her to do so, she asked him for his contacts. She demonstrated absolutely no interest in how his search unfolded or what he learned during the year-long process. He was offended on several fronts and for many legitimate reasons. She conveyed a lack of understanding and appreciation for the process of sharing information and no acknowledgment for the hard work and time he invested in making his own transition. She just wanted names. I was embarrassed, and I also lost some credibility with a valued client. He'll think twice about agreeing next time to network with one of my clients.

Getting referrals is *not* the focus of networking. It's almost as dangerous as asking for a job or for job leads. Networking is about expanding your ties. Your audience knows you're in job search. That's obvious. When you have no history with them, you risk ending a conversation quickly when you ask a yes or no question. If that's your intention, then expect to have short networking meetings if any. People don't respond well to unsupported requests. They don't like feeling that they're being used.

If Emily had been more patient and nurtured a relationship with Jack, it's likely both would have been forthcoming. In job search, information is the byproduct of a successful conversation. Your audience, whoever they may be, will generally help you if you appear to be grateful.

The Smiths: How to Make Initial Contact

Let's consider how you reach out to a networking contact. My recommendation is to send an e-mail message first and then follow-up with a phone call if you haven't heard back. Clients often challenge me on this issue: *But a letter sent through the mail will stand out.* Yes, it certainly will if you don't mind being viewed as a dinosaur. What matters most is content, not format. Why e-mail? It's fast and immediate. It also offers an excuse to make a call. Company spam filters sometimes keep messages from reaching their final destination. You need to call to make sure the message has been received: *Hi, this is Jane Smith. I just wanted to make sure that you received my e-mail.* It just makes good sense. When you have a reason to follow-through, it's a lot easier to dial the number.

You'll find many examples of correspondence in the chapter on letters. For the time being, here's one request for an informational meeting that worked. It was written by a client, Greg, a senior risk management professional. He had recently left an organization where he had worked for more than a decade. Although Greg was active in attending industry conferences and events, he was not generally focused on establishing new relationships. Being in job search was a foreign and unfamiliar experience for him. As a CFA, he was more comfortable analyzing numbers and information and less so in promoting himself. Job search forced him out of the analyst's "closet."

The e-mail begins with a reference to how you're related to the person receiving the correspondence. In the next paragraph, you provide a little background information that would be relevant and exciting to the reader or at the very least get the reader to feel that spending time with you would not be a burden. In the third paragraph, emphasize again the intention of the e-mail and offer a disclaimer. You'll see next what I mean by that. This allows you to include a resume without appearing to be asking for a job. In the last paragraph, express thanks and a strategy for following up:

Hi Jackie,

It was great to see you at the ABC Conference. As you may recall, we also met previously at —————. I was glad that John re-introduced us.

Let me explain why I am contacting you. I recently left ————— and I am in the process of speaking to colleagues in the industry. In my role as a senior —————-at —————, I was a member of a cross-functional team responsible for building ————— for the company. My principal focus was on identifying risk exposure in —————'s portfolio of structured securities, and the bulk of my time was devoted to CMBS in recent months.

My intention for the time being is solely to meet colleagues in the industry and to expand my network. ————— is at the center of many exciting ventures and would be a wonderful resource for me to make contact. To facilitate our conversation, I am attaching my resume to provide some additional background. I am not sure if you are the person I should be reaching out to and would appreciate if you would refer me to the appropriate person.

Many thanks for taking a moment to read my e-mail. These are very exciting times for —————, and I wish you the best of luck and much success! I look forward to our conversation and will follow up with you over the next couple of days.

Best regards,

Greg

Notice the tone of the e-mail. It's upbeat, clear in its intention, and assumes that a meeting will happen. It expresses gratitude for the opportunity to meet, and it's also respectful. Most important, it's a brief, quick read.

Regarding what to say in your subject line, that's a simple matter. For some reason, it seems to be one of those barriers that suck far too much time and creative energy out of networking. If you have a mutual friend who's made the referral, just reference that person. In Greg's case, the person in common was John. Here's what he could have said: *John* ————, *our mutual friend: ABC Conference.* It's my version of "string" theory, where you tie together bits of information that get the reader to both take note and to open the e-mail. If Greg and Jackie did not have John in common, here's another approach: *ABC Conference, great presentation.*

The Call

You make the call. You'll most likely reach one of three options: an assistant or gatekeeper, voicemail, or the person you sent the e-mail to. What do you say? Before you say anything, think about why you're calling:

- It's to ensure that your e-mail was received.
- It's to arrange a time to meet for informational purposes... remember, this is a networking meeting you're trying to schedule.
- It may be to provide a little background information to establish your credibility. When you sound smart, people are more inclined to feel like they'll get something out of the conversation, too...that it's not a waste of their time to speak or meet with you.

When it comes to assistants or gatekeepers, one of the few benefits of a soft market is that fewer of these people are around to protect their bosses. In any event, you still need to be prepared for a conversation with an individual whose mission is to run interference. Let's return to Jane.

Jane: Hi, this is Jane Smith. I'd like to speak to Jim.

The Assistant: Why are you calling?

Jane: I wanted to make sure that Jim received my e-mail. He's expecting to hear from me. Our mutual friend, Lori ———— ——-, made the introduction.

Keep it simple. Extraneous information is just that, and it will confuse the person you're talking to. There's no need to go into further detail unless necessary or to determine Jim's schedule so that you can follow up.

What if you get voicemail? If so, it's critical that you know in advance what you plan to say. There's nothing more embarrassing than a rambling message that gets "timed out," and then a follow-up call to see if the message was received and to leave another with the same information. Most people are far too busy to appreciate long messages. It's a burden to them, and it makes you look flakey. You need to be respectful of their time and also realize that the phone message is your very first impression. The same applies to texting. Keep it brief.

> Jim: Hello, you've reached my voicemail. Please leave a message after the tone. If you need immediate assistance, please contact —————- at —————————.

Neither Jane nor you need immediate assistance. Here's Jane's message.

> Jane: Hi Jim, this is Jane Smith. Just wanted to make sure you received my e-mail. I've been referred to you by our mutual friend, Lori —————. Briefly: Wharton MBA, the past three years at Citibank in asset management. At a turning point professionally, and Lori felt that you'd be a great person to meet. In fact, she referred to you as brilliant. Here's my number ————— and my e-mail —————————. I'll also take the liberty to follow up with you...I'm sure you're very busy. I look forward to our conversation.

When you leave a voicemail message, please make sure to speak slowly and clearly. You might also consider repeating your telephone number a second time. If you're calling from a cell phone, be mindful that messages sometimes cut out.

OK, Jane finally calls and she reaches Jim. Now what?

Jane: Jim, hi, this is Jane Smith. I'm hoping you received my e-mail. I was referred to you by our mutual friend, Lori ———— ———-. Do you have just a moment to chat?

Jim: Sure, but I only have a minute or two before my next meeting.

Jane: Thanks, I know how busy you must be. As I mentioned in my note, I'm right now considering several options professionally and Jane spoke very highly of you as someone who'd have great insight. Briefly, my background: Wharton MBA, three years at Citibank in asset management.

Jim: We're not hiring right now. In fact, we just completed a round of cuts.

Jane: Jim, let me emphasize, that's not my intention for calling. My goal right now is to meet a lot of smart people and to make sure I'm on the right track. I wonder if you might have 15 or 20 minutes to meet in person. I'll work around your schedule.

The Worst-Case Scenario

One last telephone scenario: Jane is successful in reaching Jim. He's receptive to a conversation but only by phone. In fact, he would prefer to speak at that very moment. It's always better to meet in person, but that's not necessarily an option—either the person is busy or just located too far away. If Jim is a desirable person to network with, Jane better be ready to have her networking meeting real-time. She'll need her pitch, her questions, and be clear on what she wants out of the conversation in terms of takeaways.

Jim: Hi, Jim here.

Jane: Jim, hi, it's Jane Smith. I was referred to you by our mutual friend, Lori —————————. I hope you recall receiving my e-mail. I'm thrilled to have reached you in person. Do you have a moment to chat?

Jim: It's kind of busy right now. What do you want?

Jane: As I mentioned in my e-mail, I'm right now considering several options professionally and Lori spoke very highly of you as someone who'd have great insight. I was hoping that you'd be available to meet with me for 20 minutes or so to get your thoughts on direction and strategy.

Jim: I'm delighted to speak with you, but as I just mentioned, my schedule is pretty crazy. Why don't we spend some time on the phone right now?

Jane: Great, well, my background briefly, Wharton MBA, three years in asset management at Citibank responsible for....

The lesson here: If we're targeting high-profile people to network with, especially those who are busy, they need to be convinced that the time they spend with us is time well-spent. That's why Jane gratefully accepts an initial meeting with Jim by phone, even if she'd prefer to speak at another time. She follows up with a gushing thank-you note, which will most likely lead to another phone conversation, more advice, and at some point a meeting in person. Eventually she'll wear down Jim's resistance. By then, he'll see her as a colleague and perhaps even as a quasi-friend.

Telephone Follow-Up: Format for the Call

Here's a cheat sheet to remind you how to prepare for and structure your call:

1. Who you reach and what to say:
   - Assistant or gatekeeper
   - Voicemail
   - The person you really want to speak to
2. Why you're calling:
   - To check that your resume was received
   - Explain the point of the call...a referral, in the process of..., a turning point, and so on
3. Introduction:
   - A little about you to establish credibility

4. Schedule a time to meet

5. Prepare for worst-case scenario

Bill: The Skeptic

Bill worked in back-office operations in the commodities division of a major investment bank. He joined the bank after a brief career in public accounting. It was a turning point professionally. Early on, he was assigned to work for a rising star, a charismatic fellow who acquired increasing responsibility and power. He assembled a team of smart, hard-working professionals who were willing to put their boss and the firm before their own self-interest. Their commitment and Bill's was undivided. Bill was very lucky. His boss promoted and protected him and made sure that he was rewarded generously. In return, Bill was loyal to a fault. You probably know and have worked with someone like him, the kind of guy who thinks: *If I work hard, they'll take care of me.* And they did...for a while.

It felt like Bill's world fell apart when his boss retired early from the firm. Although the details were kind of fuzzy, the decision was not entirely voluntary. So, in dividing up his universe, he was virtually powerless to ensure that his people landed safely in new homes. Besides, the group had a reputation for going a little "rogue." Bill was initially reassigned to another group reporting to a peer and then, when the next round of cuts were announced, his name was among the many on a long list.

When I met Bill, he had already been in job search for three months or so. It wasn't pretty. He had a chip on his shoulder the size of a boulder: *How could they do this to me? After I gave them everything?* He had made the mistake of assuming that an organization, which is made up of smart and dedicated people, would make a smart decision. He also believed that it would act humanely, or at the very least, it would recognize his contributions over the years. It didn't. It acted as people do—smart people—when they're forced to make a difficult decision. Someone gets caught in the political cross-fire. In this case, it was Bill and many others. It wasn't a dumb decision; it was just a decision.

Bill's job search up to that point comprised of responding to ads and calling recruiters—some of whom he had not been particularly gracious to in years past. Now he was reaching out to these same recruiters, and in large part, they were unavailable and unsympathetic. Yes, the economy had tanked, and assignments were few and far between, but it was also payback time. Bill's networking was limited to calls to a few old colleagues who were in pretty much the same position as him. Most of their conversations would eventually lead to how badly they'd been treated and how the firm had changed for the worse.

Bill had a great resume and terrific experience. What was missing was any ability or willingness to engage in self-promotion. He had never learned how, and now it felt like a foreign language. As a first step, Bill and I worked together to identify as many networking options as possible: alumni groups, professional associations, LinkedIn groups, and so on. It was a starting point. The goal was to get him one step closer to like-minded peers.

Next step, Bill and I worked on a story to explain why he was in job search and what he was looking to accomplish in networking. It was important to defuse the emotional triggers that could set him off. In truth, it wasn't my goal to understand or resolve his anger; it was only to get him focused and on track for job search. My request to him was critical: that he take the anger and find a place to warehouse it. Once he landed a new position, it was up to him if he wanted to continue to obsess. For the time being, it was off limits.

There were several issues Bill needed to address: why and when he was separated from the firm, why he remained there for as many years as he did, his career goal and qualifications, and what he was expecting and asking for in his networking meetings. It was a lot of ground to cover but all necessary information to share with his networking audience...the goal being to establish his credibility quickly. In particular, Bill was also concerned about the length of time that he had been out since leaving his firm. He was self conscious about the extended break, and as a result, his first efforts at an explanation reflected this discomfort. Getting the explanation just right took some time at first, but once he was there, the rest all fell into place. Together we crafted a brief story—actually, not much longer than 30 seconds—which incorporated each of these elements into a neat, tidy, and even playful positioning statement.

> Thanks for agreeing to spend time with me. Our mutual friend, ————, felt that you'd be a great guy to meet. By the way, she sends her best to you and hopes to see you at the ———— conference.
>
> I was with ———— for most of my career in various leadership roles in the commodities division. I'm one of those "reformed" loyal soldiers who never really appreciated the importance of building a network...better late than never! I've met some amazing people.
>
> I left the firm last year following a major re-organization. My boss retired a few months prior to my "divorce," so I sort of knew I'd be an easy mark. I took a little time off, got my finances in order, and I'm ready now to return to work. I'm hoping to get your insight on the market, people and firms to pursue, and any general advice on how to best position myself.

Why not acknowledge what you, and the person you're networking with, already know: that you didn't do what you should have—build a network—when it was the best time to do so, and that you take full responsibility now for your failure to network earlier in your career. The person you're networking with clearly sees this as an important and valuable activity, not just something you do when you find yourself stuck in a job search that feels like it will never end. Remorse and gratitude will go a long way in getting people to go above and beyond for you.

Let's consider one last point with respect to our friend, Bill. In being out there as a novice networker, he was surprised to find that phone calls and e-mails were often not returned. Even friends would occasionally fall off the radar screen. It was both surprising and frustrating for him. He assumed the worst when commitments were not honored...that the rejection was intentional. It's not. People don't follow-up for reasons we may never know and to speculate is a waste of time. It's an even bigger waste of time to blame yourself for something you have no control over. In networking, as in many other job search activities, some people will disappoint you. Those are the people you remove from your network while focusing your attention on those who help you.

If an initial e-mail and two or three follow-ups don't result in a response, it's unlikely that person is going to be helpful. However, if the person you're reaching out to is potentially a valuable resource, my recommendation is to try one last time...but this next time, you employ a slightly more aggressive and devious strategy. I refer to this as the Jewish Guilt Technique. Although it works more often than not—in fact, it's successful most of the time—it's not foolproof. Here's how it's used: You send an e-mail and hear nothing back. Then you make a couple of phone calls to make sure the e-mail was received. No response. Here's the voicemail message you leave for John, Steve, Leslie, or whoever you think has blown you off:

> Leslie, hi, this is Bill Johnson. I'm hoping you're OK. I've left a couple of messages for you and hadn't heard back. I'm really just calling to make sure you're alright. Here's my number and my e-mail...again, I'm calling just to make sure you're ok.

If you sound sincere, you'll more than likely get a response. I've also found that this technique tends to have a quick turnaround time. You've left a heartfelt, concerned, but not overly familiar message. To not respond to you, even if you're a complete stranger, would leave the person you've called feeling like a schmuck. That's our goal. When that happens, be prepared to ask for what you want.

Gary: A Good Network, A Bad Resume

Sometimes a resume cannot, and should not, stand on its own. You may be great and you may also know it, but your resume may not tell the same story. Far too much information has the potential to be lost in translation. It's not always possible to find exactly the right words to describe the various roles you've played and the contributions you've made. It's also challenging to spin what may appear to be problematic events. That's why networking is a brilliant development in how job search is managed. It allows you to explain. Unlike the old maxim about a picture speaking a thousand words, most resumes benefit from performance. A piece of paper or information presented virtually on a screen lacks context that is often necessary to smooth over rough edges or translate what is incomprehensible.

A great resume cannot disguise or hide a problem. That would be misleading. If you've been out for a long time or you left an organization that is known to be growing, you better have a good explanation. If you've hopped around, then your moves will be obvious to just about everyone who reads your resume. Even with a little bit of creative editing, they'll still be there. Even if the moves are easy to support, the resume won't do it for you. You need to explain your career in person to re-direct attention toward the value you offer.

Why focus on resumes in a chapter about networking? The more time you devote to establishing and building key relationships, the less you'll need to rely on over-used job search resources like postings and recruiters. In a tough market, these generally don't work. Recruiters don't have assignments, and postings generate hundreds or thousands of responses. On the other hand, when you network, you're in the driver's seat, and you have the power to build as many or as few of these relationships as you'd like. Besides, when people like us, they tend to overlook some of the flaws. They also help us in our job search. That's the potential that networking offers.

Gary began his career as a trader after receiving his MBA. Life before business school: He spent a year in law school followed by two long years working for a management consulting firm. Law school was a huge mistake, which anyone who knew him well could have anticipated. Even his parents discouraged him from applying. With respect to consulting, that wasn't a good match either. Gary is decisive and impatient. He zones out in meetings. He also needs to see results immediately. Although consulting offered him the intellectual rigor he desired, he felt short-changed by not being able to participate in project execution.

Gary loved the MBA program and made the most of his time there both academically and socially. He's an out-going, athletic fellow and smart, too. He makes friends easily and keeps them. He worked at several firms...first a big sell-side institution, then a few hedge funds. He jumped from one firm to another for a number of reasons, all of the moves justified at the time. But collectively after 12 years in the business, it was a challenging and long story to tell: a move with a team, a political meltdown, a bad decision, a crazy boss, a firm that was taken over, and another that wound down shortly after he joined. No matter how obvious the reasons, at some point it started to look like the moves were more about Gary and his inability to commit.

Gary grew disillusioned with the constant movement and the feeling of always needing to be one step ahead. He really didn't like being viewed as a job hopper. It's just how things seemed to play out. None of it was performance related—just timing, bad luck, and in two cases, the opportunity to make a lot more money...or so he thought at the time. He discovered, however, that with each move, he was trading down with respect to quality of firm, compensation, and stature.

Call it a premature midlife crisis, Gary decided to pursue a more entrepreneurial direction. He found a position with a registered financial advisor. It was a tough year. Although he liked the independence, he didn't see the potential to earn substantial income in a reasonable enough time frame.

Gary introduced himself to me at a career lecture for alumni of his business school. He had just recently made the decision to return to Wall Street, and he was nervous about how he would be received. With a spotty track record and a time out in an unrelated field, he had reason to be concerned.

As a first step in our work together, I asked Gary about his expectations for job search. What kind of job was he looking for and within what timeframe was he hoping to land? Was he willing and able to hold out for the right opportunity? In the past, he made several important decisions impulsively, and these ended up creating a far bigger mess than he cared to admit. With a wife and two kids now, he had a greatly reduced tolerance for risk or for failure. He needed to make a good decision. The challenge: how to best position the decision to return to trading. That meant figuring out how to offset the movement and the impression that he was a job hopper so that his network would feel comfortable putting itself on the line.

> Thanks for making yourself available. It really means a lot to me. I'm deeply grateful. As I think you know, I've got a pretty complicated history and I'm hoping to get your advice on how I can best position myself. Here's my goal: to find a trading job at either a hedge fund or a smaller sell-side institution. I'm prepared to hold out for the right opportunity. That means good people and a solid platform. I will not make a commitment until I've done my homework.

It's not your goal to present your audience with a monologue. You need to come up for air and to listen for questions, both those that are stated explicitly and those that will surface through a reaction or gesture. Too much information too soon will not get processed. Let the person you're meeting with ask for clarification or raise challenges. They deserve to be convinced that it's not a waste of their valuable time to share their resources with you. In Gary's case, it's almost a guarantee that he'd be asked about the moves: why, when, and how. I'd certainly need that information before I'd open my rolodex, and I'm sure you would, too.

It was inevitable that Gary would receive feedback in his meetings that would be critical and even discouraging. Even from friends.

Not everyone was committed to seeing him land successfully, especially in a highly competitive market. Gary could not afford to take this personally. He just had to recognize it for what it was and extract whatever value may have been gained from the meeting. No pushback and no defensiveness: *You're right. That's precisely the issue and the impression that concern me, too, and it's a real struggle.* Sometimes the best strategy is to disarm your audience by agreeing with them. You steal their thunder. In large part, though, Gary's network was supportive and helpful. That's because he'd been helpful to them in the past. For Gary, what goes around eventually came around.

The lesson here: Good relationships and a great reputation will more than offset a spotty record...as long as you tell the right story. What are the key elements in Gary's story and in yours?

- **It's brief.**   A complicated history has to be simplified for your audience. You can't allow them to get distracted by clutter or overwhelmed by detail.

- **There's intention and logic.**   What you want now must be clear, precise, and unequivocal in its message. It also needs to be supported.

- **It's sincere.**   Do you say what you mean and mean what you say? What you tell people and how you present it are equally important.

- **The information is organized in a way to facilitate its understanding.**   How the details are presented will have great bearing on how they're processed and understood by your audience.

- **You appear thoughtful and self-aware.**   It may seem obvious, but you have to show that you're clear on knowing who you are, what's happened, and how you contributed to the events as they unfolded.

- **Any drama has been omitted.**   It may be colorful in painting a more interesting picture, but it also has the potential to get your audience off-track. In fact, it introduces the possibility that you may be partially responsible for creating that drama.

- **Most important...there's nothing to hide.**   You are an open book. Transparency is essential!

Networking Checklist

1. Failure to launch: What's holding you back?

2. Attitude check:
   - Enthusiasm for your goal
   - You really want to get a job

3. Who to contact: Busy people!

4. Your pitch:
   - Who you are
   - Why you're contacting them
   - What you want
   - What you offer
   - What's in it for them? How will they benefit by spending time with you?

5. Questions to ask

6. Introduction: E-mail and telephone follow-up

7. Networking meeting follow-up

8. Keep or dump?

9. When to re-contact?

When you network, the point is to build a community of like-minded and supportive colleagues who share information and resources with you. You want to move beyond the same old crowd of friends and family. It's not one-sided. You do the same. That means staying in touch and staying on top of important developments with respect to your career and theirs. *Do you keep or do you dump them?* That's a question only you can answer based on how productive your initial meeting was. Did they encourage you, provide valuable ideas, give advice that may not have been readily available, or offer to make introductions to people and firms of interest? If you answer yes to any one of these, then they belong in your network. The challenge, however, will be in managing the logistics. A network is only as good as its potential to actively support you in your job search. If it's too large, will you be able to recontact everyone on a regular basis?

Recontact your network every two to three months. Unless you have something important to report or request, more often feels needy. If it's longer than three months, they may forget you. In Chapter 8, "Write On: Effective Career Correspondence," you'll find a couple of examples of networking correspondence. In addition to the obvious, use LinkedIn updates, a Facebook newsfeed, or a blog to keep your universe up-to-date.

7

In the Arena: Mastering the Interview

What makes an interview a success? Of course, chemistry and qualifications, but it's so much more involved and rigorous as a process. Some people are blessed with impeccable social skills and the ability to appear comfortable "winging it" in virtually any situation. Then there are the rest of us...mere mortals.

Good timing and delivery go a long way in making an initial positive impression. Organizations often look for that talent early on in getting to know a candidate, and they use that information to assess how we land on our feet. Clearly, this sort of evaluation is critical if you work in a role that requires stronger-than-average people skills such as institutional sales, investment banking, or capital-raising.

As the interview process unfolds, good communications skills and charm are valuable, but not nearly as important as fundamental skills and specialized knowledge. The scrutiny given by employers to candidates in a bear market has produced heightened expectations for the interview. The interview can be the forum where you overcome the baggage on your written resume, or it can be the resting place of your hopes and dreams for the job target you've selected. "Necessary but not sufficient" allows you to get a foot in the door, but it's just a starting point. To graduate to the next level—in other words, to be taken seriously and to not be viewed as a lightweight—requires real preparation and practice.

Whether you begin with an advantage or need to unlearn bad habits, the only way to move forward is through thoughtful preparation and repeated practice. "Winging it" has its advantages, especially if you're tight on time, but it's nearly impossible to replicate success when you haven't studied what got you there.

Now, I'm not discounting the power and potential of charm. It does, and it will make a difference; but it will only get you just so far in a challenging market. At some point over the course of your interviews, you will be evaluated on substance as well as style. With many more available candidates, that will happen earlier in the interview cycle. So yes, the right packaging is critical. You also need to convey knowledge and authority to establish your credibility.

Achieving success in your interview is a lot like a complex mathematical equation. There are multiple unknown variables: the mood and personality of the interviewer, the number of candidates who are competing for the position and their qualifications, perhaps the political history of the position and the commitment of the organization to filling it. We work to gather this information to the best of our ability. However, the process of data gathering is inefficient and imperfect, and success in an interview is also the art of the possible. You have a finite amount of time to prepare, and you need to use that time effectively.

Interview success is about executing your plan, based on sound preparation. When the interviewer connects with you and understands your answers, takes your lead, and offers encouraging body language, you'll know you've done well. You'll have invested a great deal of effort and energy to create what appears to be effortless. You will have experimented with a variety of approaches to the interview, and that practice is invaluable. Use the safety of your career counselor's office or the company of your trusted friends and advisors to practice questions, test answers, and work out the flaws in your arguments.

Inside the Interviewer's Mind

Those bad dreams where we find ourselves naked in front of the class, or freefalling, offer something true about the job interview. In a way, you *are* naked. If you're not working, you *will* be asked about the separation and why it occurred. You will be exposed if you have an incomplete answer. If you are working, you will be asked why you want to leave. You will be asked to explain your history (the "tell me about yourself" question), and if you stammer or otherwise demonstrate uncertainty about how you tell your own story, it will be noticed. Remember, you're in job search...and that means you have no excuse to be unprepared.

Most interview questions can generally be organized into one of four broad categories. In this section, we'll review interviewer behavior and the interviewer's mindset, so you understand the motives behind each of these categories of questions. This will prepare you to improvise as needed when you're feeling stuck or backed into a corner by the interviewer. If you can figure out which category your response belongs in and what the interviewer seems to be looking for, then there's a pretty good starting point as to how to go about responding. The four categories of interview questions are as follows:

- The open-ended explainer (Tell me about yourself.)
- The probing challenge (Why did you or why did you not make a decision?)
- The personality tester (Will we be comfortable with you?)
- The trial balloon (What are your expectations for the next step?)

Let's examine each of the categories in turn.

The Open-Ended Explainer

I have counseled thousands of clients, and nearly every one of them has been asked the explainer: *Tell me about yourself. Walk me through your resume. Who are you?* These are just a few of the many variations on the same theme. They're essentially all one question looking for pretty much the same type of answer.

What do you say and where do you begin? It's not that simple. Maybe there's some movement on your resume—that is, you've hopped around enough to make the interviewer suspicious and you uncomfortable responding. Or perhaps, you worked for one firm for a very long period of time, and you're not sure what's relevant. Or maybe, after a long career doing something else, you only recently started working in a role that you enjoy and want to continue working in. For example, you were a sell-side trader who moved to the buy-side and then became a portfolio manager...but only recently.

The Explainer for the Job Hopper

Tell me about yourself. I'll offer several approaches to responding to this question. Of course, just as there are many ways that this question will be asked, there are many, many possible responses. None are guaranteed to work, but the examples I'm providing have been vetted by lots of my clients who needed to explain complex situations.

Yes, your own situation is unique, as it is for everyone. However, your interviewer's expectations and mindset are fairly predictable. The difference is what keeps us career counselors in business. The examples I'll use and guidance I'll provide are general advice and may not explain your career path exactly. But the approaches we'll discuss will speak to aspects of your particular job search challenge. Each of the options illustrates an aspect of the strategy you can use.

Option 1: Anticipate the Push-Back and Address Before You're Asked

> You're probably wondering about the various moves I've made. I'd like to walk you through my resume. It's pretty straightforward.

When you take the initiative, you begin to control the message. It's a question that the interviewer is bound to raise and will want to, so you have an enormous opportunity to frame the discussion on your terms, which is a crucial advantage.

Think about where you want to begin your story. Yes, it's a story. Although you need to be truthful in every aspect of your response, any savvy professional understands that some of the details may need to be a little fuzzy to protect the innocent. We'll return to this theme later in the chapter.

Option 2: Wait Until You're Asked...Gee, It Seems Like You've Moved Around a Lot...

This question is usually asked with some degree of skepticism or a genuine concern. Your response, therefore, must neutralize the emotional aspects embedded in the question. Your interviewer will be fearful about unknown variables in your situation.

I'm glad you asked.... No, never ever use that expression. You're not pleased. In fact, you're probably annoyed that yet again the issue has re-surfaced. You don't really want to talk about your sordid job hopping, do you?

An alternative may go something like the following: *Yes, it may seem that way based on a quick read of the resume. There's obviously a story behind the moves, and I do believe that having some context is critical to understanding why the moves have happened.*

Option 3: The Sincere Strategy

> My goal now at this point in my career is to find a home, and I'm prepared to hold out until that happens. I agree. There's been some movement on the resume. There's an explanation for each of the moves, and I'd be happy to walk you through my resume. I believe that having context is invaluable.

First of all, if you can't really afford to hold out or really don't want to, you either modify the explanation or accept it. Know that you may also be challenged on your determination not to work, which may seem a little odd to the interviewer in a market where any job is considered a good job. Alternatively, if you're interviewing with a firm and it's not your dream job, BUT you really need a salary, this explanation can work like a charm. They think you're holding out for them!

This is what I refer to as a "turning point" explanation. You've invested a great deal of time and energy in making this decision. Now you want to convey its magnitude and importance.

Notice also how I've used "minimizing" language to soften the bad message: *some movement.* I've used positive, upbeat language to enhance the important themes I want to support: *happy, invaluable,* and so forth.

The Explainer for the "Lifer"

If you've worked for one firm for a significant period of time—at least five years and certainly ten years or more—I'll pose two scenarios to guide your thinking. You've been in pretty much the same position for the entire time, give or take expanded responsibilities and more important-sounding titles. It's essentially the same job. Alternatively, you've had the opportunity to move around within the firm and to wear a number of hats, some interesting and one or two not so great. Maybe you've also had an overseas assignment. How do you explain your career either as a straight line along the same arc or as a series of assignments?

One Company/One Job

Always, always present your career as one that's been deeply meaningful and important to you. If it hasn't been, why would you stay in the same job for what appears to be forever? The implication is that you're either risk averse, maybe lacking in ambition, or just lazy. That's not the impression you want to make...ever...even if it's the truth. Depending on your goal, being an expert and having deep subject matter expertise should be considered assets and used to your advantage.

> I've had the good fortune to work with —— for 20 years. Gee, where did the time go? They've offered me multiple opportunities to move around, but I've really enjoyed becoming an expert in ——- and serving as a mentor to new associates. As a result, I'm often invited to speak at industry conferences, and I've assumed a leadership role in our professional association. I've also written quite a few articles. I'd be happy to send you a link to a few and to provide other writing samples.

One Company/Many Jobs

I'll offer two scenarios both describing individuals who worked for the same company for many years. Despite the overlap in their length of employment and the fact that they had similar functional roles, each situation is unique and needs to be addressed differently.

Sarah worked for a major investment bank for 12 years. She began her career as an analyst out of undergraduate school, left to get her MBA, returned as an associate in institutional sales, moved next to an administrative role as a business manager for the division, and then was asked to move to London to help start up a new business as the chief administrative officer. Are you still with me? When she returned to headquarters in New York two years later, many of her former colleagues had already left the firm. So when the cuts happened, Sarah was an easy mark. How to explain the separation?

First of all, I'm genuinely delighted to be here and to meet with you. I've been looking forward to our conversation.

Now if Sarah is interviewing for an administrative position:

With respect to my background, I'm a senior administrative executive and have worked in a range of leadership roles at the firm. I've been responsible for supporting existing main lines of business, and I've also been selected to start up high-growth and highly visible initiatives both in the U.S. and overseas.

Then Sarah talks some about her responsibilities and highlights a few of her accomplishments. *For example....*

At this point, if there's a lull or break in the conversation or the interviewer just doesn't engage, then Sarah might offer the following:

I actually joined ―― out of undergraduate school. I was recruited on campus for the firm's two-year analyst program in investment banking and then went on to business school. I rejoined the firm as an associate in institutional sales. It didn't take me long to realize that my personality and skills were much better suited to administration and project management. I was asked to join a business process team for the division. There weren't many of us from the "line" who had both hands-on experience and the temperament or patience to work in a project management capacity. It was a win-win situation from the very start, and I found myself really thriving and loving the work. The rest is history.

If Sarah has decided to return to institutional sales:

You must be wondering why I'm here. It's my goal to return to institutional sales and I'm committed to making that happen. How did I end up as the chief administrative person for this division? I'll give you the shorthand version and spare you the details.

I was asked by senior management to join a division-wide committee to help re-engineer and re-focus the business. As a result of my role on the committee, I was then asked by senior management to take on what, at the time, was supposed to be a short-term project. I thought it was great exposure to my colleagues across the company and globally and to some of the more challenging business issues we were facing. I was also reassured that my job would be there when the project was completed...so it seemed like a "no brainer."

Sarah then describes the project: its scale and scope, the organization and timing of the project, the people involved, and the issues addressed. That explained briefly, she then explains how events unfolded:

It was a pretty big home run, and I was then asked to replicate this success in London for a newly established business. Again, we knocked the cover off the ball. In taking the assignment, I made it clear that my goal was always to return to sales. Fast forward a year later, I returned to New York. Virtually all of my colleagues had left the firm by then and I found myself without a home or a rabbi. So when the cutbacks were announced, I was disappointed but not entirely surprised.

If Sarah is asked how she feels about the separation:

I learned an important lesson about trust: It's essential to trust your colleagues, but you also have to be smart when it comes to protecting and managing your career. Next time, I'll make sure that any promises and commitments are written.

No bitterness expressed. Sarah recognizes that the responsibility for creating a safety net was hers. Would she have liked the events to have worked out in her favor? Of course, and it's OK to express her disappointment both with herself and with the organization. Notice that Sarah didn't really answer the question directly. She implied how she felt about the situation, but she didn't belabor the discussion. In fact, she re-directed the focus away from the company to herself.

What about the inevitable question regarding her client relationships? She worked as an institutional salesperson, but she'd been away from her clients in an official capacity for three years. In going out on interviews, that issue was raised again and again. If I were a hiring manager, I would certainly want to know how she's going to make money for me. Like all of the other questions Sarah and I anticipated, she was prepared to respond:

> I've known from the very start that I would eventually return to sales. That's been my goal and that's why I've maintained relationships with just about all of my clients. And being in London, I've also had the advantage of being introduced to an entirely new community of investors. I feel like I bring so much more now to my role as a salesperson. I'd be happy to give you a list of some of the people and firms who've agreed to work with me.
>
> There's another benefit that's not quite as obvious but I see as being invaluable. In my administrative roles, I've been directly responsible for handling a range of client service and operational matters. So I'm a lot smarter now in terms of surrounding the client. I really get what they need and want and most important how to take care of them. From my perspective, that translates into sales.

It was a successful explanation for several reasons. First and foremost, it showed that Sarah was still a "player." She maintained many of her client relationships, and she had never been too far from the business.

Sarah's colleague, Jennifer, worked for the same institution for 16 years. Unlike Sarah, she dropped out of college after three semesters and then joined the firm as an administrative assistant supporting a fixed income marketing team. She completed her undergraduate degree at night, and over time she was promoted to analyst, associate, and then vice president. It also helped that Jennifer's boss was considered a rising star. As his reputation and world grew, she took on increasing responsibilities and, at some point that she could barely remember by now, she moved into a marketing leadership role. She was one of two employees sponsored by division senior management for an executive

MBA program—in the office Monday through Thursday and in classes Friday and Saturday. She was working around the clock.

It felt to Jennifer as if she had stepped into an artificial reality. She could not have imagined that her life and career would lead her down this path and that she would experience such good fortune. The firm was not known for its generosity, so, for Jennifer, the firm's paying for the MBA and supporting her time out of the office demonstrated a real commitment to her and her career. Jennifer would later realize that working hard and getting results is fulfilling your side of the employment contract, and when you work hard, you deserve to be rewarded. Tuition reimbursement isn't a gift or "a commitment." It's compensation.

Shortly after Jennifer graduated from business school, she had a long talk with her mentor, who was now a top executive, as well as with the senior administrative officer for the division. They were serious conversations about next steps and her future. Jennifer shared her growing restlessness in her role and the desire to experience life elsewhere in the firm...possibly moving to asset management or a more dramatic shift to corporate philanthropy. She thought the latter area would represent a nice balance between commerce and good works. It wasn't an ultimatum, just a wish list. Now that she was an MBA—an executive MBA, for that matter—it was a reasonable request, right?

A month or so later, as part of a large downsizing in her division, Jennifer was advised that she was being made redundant. What the ...! She was devastated. How could this have happened to her? How could they have done this? Didn't the MBA show how valuable she was, and would continue to be, to the firm?

First of all, "they" is meaningless. Who are "they": an organization? It was an organizational decision, not a personal one. Jennifer was presuming that an investment bank, particularly hers, would act humanely based upon how she had been treated in the past. Not! Investment banks don't focus on history. They're only concerned with the present, and what needs to happen to ensure that revenue continues and bonuses are paid out. If it means reducing headcount, so be it. Those folks or others can be re-hired when profitability is restored. However presumptuous or naïve, Jennifer thought she was safe because of her ties to senior management. Unlike her colleagues, she also felt that she was different, even better. At the very least, she deserved to be treated with compassion and to be evaluated based upon her history at the firm and her relationships there. There had to be another job for her.

Jennifer reached out to her former boss. He was now many levels removed. Although friendly and concerned, and fond of her, he explained that this was a business decision. His hands were "tied." She no longer worked for him, and he had many other more pressing challenges to manage. Certainly, he would serve as a reference...but even here he cautioned her about the bank's official policy regarding references and not having worked with her in many years. What happened to loyalty and the benefits of hard work?

Lesson: In a climate and market where jobs are few and far between, cutbacks at investment banks are often made to achieve immediate, measurable bottom-line results. Expressing dissatisfaction or a desire to move is like wearing a sign that says "fire me." Look for career direction outside the firm, from a professional like a career counselor who knows the Street or from friends, not from your boss.

How does Jennifer explain her divorce from the firm? In a word: easily. It's a simple story to tell. She needed to position herself using the best of her experience and relying heavily on her good reputation. But first, before she could explore life outside the firm, the dust had to settle over her involuntary separation. Jennifer experienced a profound sense of loss, as well as anger, disappointment, and bitterness. This reaction is entirely understandable after an illustrious and exciting 16 years. For Jennifer, it was critical that she understand and manage her feelings so that they would not creep unexpectedly into her interviews.

So Jennifer, why did you leave the firm? What happened?

I've had an amazing career at —————; in fact, it's been life changing. Until recently, I was a Vice President in ————— where I was responsible for —————, —————, and —————. I was also sponsored for Columbia's executive MBA program, which I just completed last May. I was one of only two employees sponsored by the division.

I'm sure you must know that we've had several waves of cuts in my division as well as across the organization. I had a pretty good hunch that I was vulnerable. I'd had several conversations with our senior management team just prior to and after completing the MBA, and they knew I was eager to make a change. So yes, I was an obvious candidate for the separation. In truth, when I look at this objectively, which is not always easy to do, why save me when someone else really wants to be here doing this job?

Yes, it's disappointing, but not a big surprise.

Being truthful in an interview is always recommended over dishonesty. Sometimes, however, the details need to be scrubbed so that you position yourself in the very best possible light. In Jennifer's case, it was good for her to convey that she was in the proverbial driver's seat...that she was in control of her destiny. She and I worked closely to ensure that the story focused on the following three core themes:

- The fact that the bank had sponsored her for a very expensive and time-consuming MBA program offered to only a select few. This implied she was highly valued, so any decision to cut her would have been a very difficult one for the bank and one that was made reluctantly.

- Jennifer was ready for a change and shared this information with key people. This information, no doubt, was taken into account in making the decision.

- That Jennifer, like the rest of us is human, and yes, it was a big disappointment to be terminated.

Probing Challenge

As we've said, interview questions can be organized into four types. So far, we've covered the "explainer": *Tell me about yourself*. Often, after the explainer, the second category of interrogation is not far behind, when the interviewer probes into your decision making. *Why? Why not?* This is called question "creep." When you share information, it is inevitable that new questions will arise and the information you provide will overlap. As Sarah and Jennifer discovered, an incomplete explanation may confuse the interviewer, especially a tenacious one who's determined to get at the truth. I'm expecting that you'll tell the truth, too. But sometimes the truth just needs to be better organized before it's ready for prime time.

More often than not, these questions focus on why something didn't happen or if it did, why it broke down. Here are some examples:

- You only worked for how long at that company?
- Gee, you seem to have moved around quite a bit. Why?
- I don't see a graduation date from your school...when was that?
- It looks like you didn't graduate from college? Why?
- When did you leave your last job?
- Why you (versus anyone else at your company) if you've been fired?
- How could you have possibly made that decision? (Whatever that decision may be; just fill in the blanks. We all have our own crosses to bear.)

Interviewers question us to get to know who we are and whether or not they or, in the case of recruiters, their clients, would like to work with us. It's in their interest that they dig beneath the surface to uncover any potential problems, issues, or sources of embarrassment. Wouldn't you? That's what Danny discovered when he lost his job at a big brokerage house.

Danny was hired into back-office operations right out of undergraduate school. A former college athlete and fraternity member, he had the right pedigree and personality to move quickly—within two years—to an assistant trading position and a year later to trader. He played on the company basketball and softball teams. He was invited often to join more senior colleagues for drinks. You get it. He was well-liked...but not enough to avoid getting the axe only six months after his promotion. It wasn't due to performance. His firm decided to exit the business, and the entire team was eliminated. Despite the public announcement, Danny still found himself being grilled by interviewers. If he was so great, why did the firm let him go? Couldn't they have found another home for him?

So, Danny, tell us about your background.

I trade —————. I joined ————————— right out of college, and it's been an amazing experience for me. If it's helpful, I can walk you through my resume.

Danny worked a grand total of 3.5 years and for only six months as a trader. Neither is very long in terms of time and exposure, which has immediate impact on his potential to add value. How much would he be able to contribute and how soon? Because his experience is relatively light, the intention here is to establish and enhance his credibility and authority by stretching out the story. That generally happens by starting out at the beginning and walking your audience through the entire chronology. Danny then gives examples of his knowledge of the products, his certifications, the names of more senior and well-respected colleagues, and any other relevant information, such as his plans to sit for the CFA exam.

If the interviewer observes: *But you've only traded for six months?*

Yes, that's right. I was given a lot of responsibility early on and some amazing opportunities. I also had a few great teachers and mentors: —————, —————, and —————. Having spent my first two years behind the scenes, I got to know a lot of people, and I paid very close attention to what makes a trader successful.

If you make a statement like the last one, then you better be prepared to back it up. If you're called on it, make sure you sound smart, thoughtful, and in Danny's case, mature. Maybe he talks about a few of those characteristics and then he adds:

> I'm a really good trader, but I don't take that for granted. I know I'll need to prove to you that I have the experience, the qualifications, and the commitment. And if I need to, I'm definitely willing and prepared to come on board in a more junior role.

> I'm committed to working hard. I'm also happy to provide you with references from some people who've been in the business for a long time...you may know them.

The strategy for Danny is best described as eager, hungry, and smart. Know both your assets *and* liabilities when you prepare for interviews. It's guaranteed that a good interviewer will focus on the latter for all of the right reasons. They want to feel confident in knowing that you're the best possible candidate and that there will be no unexpected surprises.

How do you assess the vulnerable aspects of your resume? I recommend a simple exercise I refer to as the "resume audit." Identify a group of, say, five or six people who you respect professionally and whose judgment you trust. Think of this as the equivalent of a focus group but not one where everyone meets together. Ask each of them to review your resume independently and position your request as follows:

> Thanks for agreeing to review my resume. I'm actually not looking for feedback on the resume per se. My goal is to figure out where all the potential land mines may be in terms of my background. That way, I can best prepare to address these points when I'm actually in the interview. I figure that if you find them, then it's highly likely others will, too. I'm grateful for any feedback. Let me emphasize that it will be accepted without any defensiveness on my part.

The point is to get feedback that's not sugar coated. If the advisors you've assembled know that you won't debate with them, then they're much more likely to take the time to fully review the document and give you their honest reactions. Whether you agree with them or not, you need their feedback to prepare a defensible strategy. I can assure you that if there's a red flag on the resume, someone is bound to see it.

A while back, I was working with a fellow named John. He and his wife were both institutional salespeople for money center banks. Shortly before John and I were introduced, his wife had their second child. They decided that it was the right time for one of them to stay at home with the kids. John's wife, Stacy, was a bigger producer than him. He also had an idea for a new business that they were both convinced he could pursue from home. The path to hell is often paved with good intentions or, in this case, a half-baked business plan and a naïve understanding of the role of stay-at-home-parent. They also didn't take into account a strategy for re-entry should John want to or need to return to work.

Even in the best of times, Wall Street treats controversial decisions like John's status as a stay-at-home father with skepticism and disbelief. *It's unthinkable! How could he have made such a stupid decision! He must have really screwed up in his last job!* After a respectable effort, John realized his business was going nowhere. Nor did he discover that he was well-suited to be a full-time parent. He and Stacy agreed that it made sense for him to return to work. After John had bombed in virtually all of his interviews, he ended up with me. He had one big opportunity remaining, and he was nervous about making a good impression. "Nervous" was actually an understatement. He was terrified. He felt like he had used up virtually all of his contacts.

What's worse, John didn't call me until the day before his interview! We scheduled a meeting for early the next morning. It was battlefield triage for his resume and interview. With only an hour to prepare him, he and I performed a resume audit. I de-constructed the resume line by line. No date, skill, or experience was sacred. It was my intention to come up with a short list of the most obvious questions he could be asked and to make sure he was prepared to respond. I wanted him to make an overwhelmingly positive impression.

What were some of the questions?

- At the very top of the list: *You decided to do what?*
- You've been out for three years; what happened to your book of business...your clients?
- Why did you leave your last position?
- If you wanted to be an entrepreneur, how do we know you're committed to being back in a traditional organization?
- We're concerned about your skill set. A lot has changed in three years.

In every one of his meetings so far, John was grilled on his decision to exit the industry. That's where we focused our attention. I was convinced that his answers to the other questions could easily be wrapped into his story about the last three years...as long as that story was believable. In general, it's my belief that it's always better to run interference than to wait to be ambushed. Why not steal the interviewer's thunder? Anticipate the interviewer's principal concerns and make them a part of your explanation.

The approach works as follows:

- Consider the possible trouble spots, hopefully, based upon a thorough audit of your resume and reflection on past interviews.
- Strategize on how to weave the various elements together.
- Practice, practice, and practice telling the story.
- Get feedback from your resume audit team on the story.

- Present the story as if it's no big deal, that the decision was an obvious one given the circumstances at the time and your expectations for a successful outcome.
- Make sure you don't come across as arrogant, impulsive, or short-sighted.
- Never apologize.

Of course, the preceding bullets are general guidelines. They'll help to explain a lot of situations but not all. You have to "own" your story and situation. I'll share with you John's story. Please bear in mind that it worked for him. It may not work for you. It's not a one-size-fits-all approach:

> I was expecting that you'd have some questions about my decision to take some time off. A lot of events coincided that led me to consider what was a huge decision for me at the time.

The point here: It was a decision that was made based upon careful, thoughtful evaluation and discussion...it was not made lightly. The more you can support the decision with solid defensible reasons—those that are based on good judgment and real-life events—the more convincing the story will be. A defensible strategy is not the same as appearing defensive. Your goal is to give the impression of being open and honest, and to do so without any overt or subliminal message that you view the interviewer as an opponent.

> We'd gone through numerous cuts at the bank, I'd been there for ten years, and the severance packages that were being offered to those of us who volunteered to leave were pretty attractive. For a long time I'd also been intrigued by the idea of starting a business, which I figured would happen either now or never. And last, but not least, I've left out probably the most important reason: We'd just had our second kid, and I really wanted to enjoy them while they were young.
>
> It's been a great couple of years and I wouldn't have changed a thing. But I really do miss the business. I've made a point to stay in touch with colleagues and clients and I've also stayed

on top of changes in the industry. Surprisingly, and I hadn't really thought much about this when I left the bank, I'm lonely working on my own. I miss being part of a team and having the resources and credibility of a big institution behind me.

Notice the tone here sounds upbeat, confident, and satisfied, not arrogant in any way. The decisions were made for all the right reasons, and now the decision to move forward is being made with the same commitment.

If the interviewer doesn't question John about making a controversial decision three years before, I can assure you it's not an oversight. It may just be that the interviewer has already formed a bias that will certainly influence how John is viewed as a candidate. If that's the case, it's even more important now for John to explain himself in a way that enhances his credibility. He needs to take a proactive approach and introduce both the decision he made and the events that preceded and followed.

You may be wondering about my decision to leave the bank three years ago. It's really one of the biggest and most difficult decisions I've ever made.

At that point, he resumes the story: *We'd gone through numerous cuts....*

Later in the day, John called me. He met with the head of sales, and what was the first question he was asked? You got it! What were you thinking when you decided to stay home? John nailed the question because he and I spent an hour or so that very morning preparing his response. John covered all the bases and more. When that happens, the interviewer just moves on to talk about the more important stuff. It becomes a non-issue. There's no need to dig any deeper.

The Personality Tester

As the interviewer moves beyond the facts, figures, resume, and background, he or she will begin testing, questioning, and discussing issues that will help them get a feel for your personality—that you have the right temperament, that your personality is well-suited to both the role and the organization, and most important, that you're the kind of person your new boss will enjoy managing and working with. It is never foolproof as a screening technique. A good candidate can and should be able to outsmart the interviewer...not to be intentionally devious but to make sure that the decision about hiring you is one that you participate in.

One age-old and popular example of this category is the "strengths and weaknesses" question. For some reason, clients seem to be uncomfortable sharing this sort of information. This is an odd reaction; it is an interview, isn't it? I'm not sure why, but it seems like the tendency when asked about strengths and weaknesses is to offer a stock answer such as: *I'm a workaholic* or *I push my people too hard* or *I'm a "people" person.* By all means, feel free to use a stock response but also know that you'll risk sounding like lots of other candidates. If the point of the interview is to distinguish yourself for the right reasons, then you've failed. You've done nothing to show your depth of self-awareness or your ability to translate your talents and unique abilities into a meaningful and thoughtful response.

The prevailing logic has been to turn a weakness into an asset and to have a strength support your qualifications as a candidate. That's not enough. On its own and without some context, your response has the potential to sound silly. Think about this for a moment: You've just disclosed a very personal piece of information. If you've shared an example of a weakness, then the person interviewing you will need to have some idea how that weakness is manifest. If it were me, I'd want to know how you dealt with it. I'd also need to be reassured that it is in no way an ongoing issue and that there's been some learning along the way.

That's why you need to take it to the next level. If the interviewer asks you about a weakness, give a real weakness. Just make sure you're not providing information that will diminish your attractiveness as a candidate or suggest an inability to perform your responsibilities. When you offer an example of your strengths, make sure to use an illustration here, too. How else will I know and believe that it's a real strength and one that can be replicated?

Keith

After graduating from a small New England liberal arts college, Keith joined a major Wall Street firm as a trainee in its operations division. He knew virtually nothing about finance, but the idea of working in New York City and making lots of money was intoxicating. Whether or not he would actually like the work was another matter entirely. That didn't seem to be all that important at the time...so career satisfaction was not a reason for concern or much examination. He had always been a strong student, and as part of his longer-term strategy, he planned to return to school at some undetermined point in the future. It was just unclear what path of study he would pursue or when.

Keith remained at the firm for almost 20 years. For the first 15, he received many promotions and he earned substantial bonuses. Without having a reason to return to school and not wanting to disrupt his cash flow he was by and large a happy camper. When the markets softened, however, Keith hit a brick wall in year 16. His firm had been reorganized, and he found himself aligned with the wrong leadership team. Many of his colleagues were separated involuntarily, and Keith was assigned to a staff position. He toiled away in this relatively obscure role, hoping to make it through the downturn. That never happened. The markets continued to spiral downward and Keith's position was eventually eliminated.

Keith viewed his staff position as a sign of failure, and in his last four years behind the scenes, he grew increasingly frustrated and angry. When the separation finally occurred, he felt tremendous relief combined with an almost blinding rage. How could they—the company—have done this to him after so many years of loyal service? What about all the hours he invested and the rest of his life that he had neglected while building his so-called career? He blamed the situation on the worst that happens in a political organization. Not knowing what else to do, he chose to do nothing. Initially this seemed like the right decision: Take some time off, enjoy life, and get back into shape. A year later, he still had no clear plan of action and no visible source of income.

Keith finally rallied and began to job search in earnest. It was an awkward process initially. He felt that the "truth" needed to be shared, and for Keith, that meant going into some detail about his unfair and untimely termination. It made for a colorful and generally unsuccessful interview. What Keith viewed as the facts came across as bitterness and unresolved anger. Although there are many examples of Keith's various rants during the early interviews, his response to the "personality" question offers unique insight into his particular challenges. By addressing the personality question, we were able to develop a more upbeat approach to many of the other questions he would be asked.

So, Keith, what do you view as your biggest weakness?

> I hate corporate politics. I'm lousy at it, and I'm just not engineered to navigate within a highly political organization. Far too much time and energy are devoted to self promotion, and it's usually the laziest and weakest members of the team who add absolutely no value or benefit to the organization. My belief has generally been that if you work hard and keep your nose to the grindstone, you'll get rewarded. That doesn't seem to be the case anymore. Nowadays, you'll get screwed.

To Keith's credit, he was providing a real weakness. It was just not packaged in a way that demonstrated real insight into managing a challenging situation or his potential to grow personally. It was a mess of an answer, as were most of Keith's responses that were more personal in nature. He was a victim, and that made everyone uncomfortable. He crossed the line from objective observation to an accusatory and very subjective, perhaps paranoid, view of the world. We all know that political behavior is a part of working in organizations of all size. To not understand politics at this point in the game was inexcusable. It also made him come across as extremely naïve.

Keith's low political IQ—his lack of political intelligence—was a real weakness and it deserved to be discussed. It's just how he was presenting it that got him into trouble again and again. As was the case in how Keith positioned most of his responses to interview questions, it was poorly thought out and in large part represented what he wanted to say rather than what he thought the audience would need to hear. That's where the learning begins to happen. I videotaped a practice interview, and Keith was shocked when we reviewed it together. He had no idea how much baggage he was carrying into the interview. Our goal then was to defuse the anger and present a more balanced and thoughtful perspective on how and why Keith found himself at this particular turning point in his career.

Let's re-play the weakness question: *Keith, what do you view as your biggest weakness?*

> I've never been much of a corporate politician. Although I realize that politics exists in all organizations, my strategy has always been to work hard and produce the highest level and quality of work. But that's not always the best strategy, as I've discovered. I've also realized that some level of political behavior may be necessary to highly functioning organizations. Of course, it's just human nature to protect your interests and to not acknowledge that is potentially dangerous. It's also a little naïve to believe that integrity only comes in one shape or size.

If Keith was so inclined, at this point he could offer an example of a challenging situation he faced and how it was addressed. It's not necessary since his response already implies an awareness of his weakness and some insight into how he's changed. It just may add further depth to the response:

> I recently found myself caught in a situation involving two teams competing for the same goal. It was an awkward position to find myself in for the following reasons....

As Keith discovered, the interview is not intended to be an exorcism. It's not a reason to bash your former employer or colleagues, or to be used as an excuse from taking responsibility for any breakdowns that may have occurred at work. The "personality" question is meant to probe for your insight and self-awareness. It may also probe for appropriateness. Do you demonstrate good judgment under pressure? Faced with a challenge, will you make choices that are thoughtful, logical, and suggest a complexity to the way you reach a decision? Will you also formulate that response within a reasonable timeframe? Even the best candidates occasionally get so nervous in an interview that they lose all perspective. That's when the balance of power shifts and the interview tanks.

The Trial Balloon

At some point in just about every interview, you'll be asked the "what next" question. You already shared detailed information on your background and qualifications. You explained why decisions were or were not made. You offered insight into your personality and hopefully avoided the inevitable traps one can easily step into.

You have yet to talk about the future. That's where you envision how your career will unfold or what sort of compensation you may be expecting. Think money, commitment, a sense of purpose, ambition. There are an infinite number of variations on the "what next" theme. Your goal is to get the interviewer to see you as more than just a candidate for a job. Are you a good fit, and do you want it?

When this category of question is asked, it's likely that you've prepared a response to the obvious: salary or where you see yourself. Let me make one point clear: This category of question is not meant to stump you. Knowing what you want, and having it aligned with what your interviewer wants and needs, is a very powerful building block in your relationship. It should not produce stress for you. The intention is to provide valuable information about how you see yourself in the world and, more specifically, in the organization. Hopefully, your long-term vision includes the organization, and that vision also conveys realistic expectations with respect to compensation. The irony: It's a one-sided evaluation because most companies operate over a very short timeframe. Unfair or not, that's what you're working with. Your loyalty must outweigh and outshine theirs.

"What next" covers an infinite range of questions that focus on the future. Compensation and commitment are two obvious areas that are often probed. Commitment may be more easily recognized as: "Where do you see yourself in three, four, or five years?" Other themes include: career development, a return to school, relocation, and so on. I've devoted substantial air time to issues around compensation in the negotiation chapter. Please refer there for best practices and recommended approaches. For really important negotiation matters, it's a good idea to seek the advice of a skilled advisor, someone who's worked extensively in navigating highly complex and often very sensitive negotiation discussions. This is not the time to cut corners. If you short-change yourself at a critical moment like this, what you don't know now may cost you dearly over the long term.

So...where do you want to be in three, four, or five years? It's not an unreasonable question. If I were interviewing you, I'd want to know how serious you are about your career and how realistic your expectations may be. Clearly, no one has the power to predict or control the future. Far too much can happen between now and then. But have you thought through the various options and opportunities that are potentially available to you and how you intend to use them to achieve your goals? That's what I'm really after when I ask that question.

Let's make it even simpler: What do you want to do? It's a perfectly harmless and reasonable question to most of us. Yes? Not so for Steve. He was the number-two person in private banking for a large global institution. He'd been there for most of his career. When the separation happened, he was filled with extremes: anger, relief, confusion, and embarrassment, to list just a few of the many emotions he experienced. Although the last two years there were not good ones, he never thought of himself as existing outside the institution. It took a while for the dust to settle, and when it did, Steve was utterly directionless. He knew that private banking would be an obvious direction to pursue, but he also felt that this would be the perfect opportunity to try something new. He had already received a few calls from recruiters and friends about private banking jobs. It was the "low-hanging fruit" dilemma. Should he take some time off to explore his options or settle for the familiar?

Here's the plan that Steve and I agreed on. He would follow up on all requests for interviews, and at the same time, he would begin to explore new directions. It didn't feel right to Steve, but he needed practice on both fronts. Job search at his level, and for an equivalent position, could take months to manage successfully. He would benefit the most by exploring new options, evaluating the barriers to entry in a new field, and then if faced with a decision, he would have a basis to either move forward on the offer or continue to explore this new direction.

Steve was essentially an interview virgin. He conducted hundreds of interviews over the years, but it seemed like a lifetime ago that he joined the bank. It was. The year before, he celebrated his 25th anniversary, and during that entire time, he had not once flirted with the possibility of life outside. Even recruiter calls were either ignored or passed along to colleagues. As a first step, he began to network. The goal was twofold. He would gather information about opportunities in private banking, *and* seek out advice of smart people as to new directions. That's where the process broke down. It was the "what next" question that tripped him up.

So, Steve, what do you want to do next?

I'm not sure yet. I was in private banking for most of my career, and that's pretty much the world that I know.

For a fellow with an amazing track record and impressive credentials, this was a rather anemic response. People wanted and expected more from him. It wasn't that they needed Steve to know exactly what he wanted next (that was the point of networking, wasn't it?), they wanted to be reassured that he was decisive about the process if not the end goal. Here's how he repositioned his request:

I'm at a turning point professionally. I can continue to do what I do well and enjoy. I can also consider alternatives. I've been given this gift...time to reflect on my career, to consider options, and to figure out if I'm on the right track. I know it's a tough market, but I'm willing to take a little time to think this through. That's precisely why I'm so excited to talk with you. I know you'll have real insight into two of the areas that I'm most interested in: family offices and wealth management.

That's where Steve needed to start his conversation...with confidence and clarity. Once he got comfortable with the idea of being in job search, he made that his mission. He approached each networking meeting knowing exactly what he wanted to accomplish at that particular moment in time.

Awkward Interview Questions

These are the questions that give you sweaty palms and keep you awake night after night. They're not necessarily inappropriate or unexpected. They just make you feel like the interviewer is trying to trip you up or that you'll disclose something horrible about yourself.

One question that's often asked is guaranteed to produce anxiety: *Who else are you talking to?* It's an interview question that seems to ask for more than it's willing to give back. It's also one-sided and weighted heavily in favor of the interviewer. In addition to touching on issues of discretion, good judgment, and trust, it's often asked when you already feel vulnerable just by virtue of being in job search. You're the candidate; they're the interviewer. How do you respond without appearing overly secretive, paranoid, or defensive? On the other hand, how do you maintain an upbeat and positive impression (translation: so you don't screw up the interview) if you refuse to respond? In the best of times, this sort of question feels invasive and unnecessary. In a tough market, providing this information would be dumb. Never tell them who else you're talking to. **Let me repeat:** Never tell them who else you're talking to!

Diane is a compliance attorney. She was given three months' advance notice by her boss, the COO of a mid-sized hedge fund, that her position would be eliminated. The separation was not performance related. In fact, that's why she was given a "heads up" in confidence. The firm's partners felt bad about the decision and wanted her to get a jump start on job search. The fund lost several billion dollars through redemptions, a lousy market, and a few bad investment decisions. There wasn't much to go around, and it was unlikely the situation would turn around. Everyone liked her, but just not enough to pay to keep her there.

Diane began to network immediately. She knows a lot of people and keeps in touch with them. She's also been helpful over the years to professional colleagues in job search. It was payback time: They owed her now. Obvious questions were raised and anticipated: Why do you want to leave your firm, what are you looking for, what was your compensation, and what is your expectation regarding compensation? These questions were asked by interviewers and, occasionally, by people with whom she was networking. Yes, the money questions were a little nervy. But we figured that she should expect colleagues in her industry not to follow the rules, the appropriate protocol for what questions are acceptable and which are off limits. That's why we spent considerable time evaluating, preparing, and structuring the various responses.

Diane is unflappable. She doesn't get flustered easily—most likely a by-product of working for several years with traders combined with her Brooklyn roots. She called me one evening and unleashed a long string of expletives about a meeting she had earlier in the day. She was furious. The interviewer asked her where else she was interviewing. It caught her off guard, and she ended up sharing far too much information. How should Diane have responded?

> I'd be happy to share that information with you...but not right now. I'm sure you can understand how competitive the market is and how valuable this information has the potential to be. It's taken a monumental effort to identify and nurture these opportunities. Once we've moved further along in our conversations, of course, I'd be happy to tell you who else I'm talking to. In fact, when an offer is presented, I'd want you to know so anyone you might know in job search can benefit, too.

Alternatively, you and Diane can take a slightly different approach. It's what I refer to as the "I'd really like to but my hands are tied" strategy:

> I'd be happy to share that information with you, but I've been asked by several of the firms I'm talking to not to go public yet. They're concerned about being overwhelmed by resumes...so I have to respect their request. I'm sure that once we've moved further along, that shouldn't be an issue. In the meantime, I can certainly tell you about the firms in general and more specifically about the opportunities.

It's always easier to blame a third party when you're asked for something you don't want to or shouldn't provide. In truth, the information that's been requested is most likely available to everyone. You've worked hard to obtain it, so don't be quick to give it up.

Rob: What Happened and Why?

One of my clients, Rob, was faced with a challenging, and in hindsight, very obvious interview hurdle. It was a challenge he and I should have anticipated early on, but for a variety of reasons, it was not addressed. Rob is an options trader with a decent track record. What do I mean by decent? In his particular situation, he had outstanding performance but far too much movement on his resume. As a career coach and advisor on strategy, that nets out as decent...a B minus. While you're making money, the hopping is never a problem. But when you hit an extended stretch of bad luck, it's the movement that people focus their attention on. They don't like it. It makes them uncomfortable. Although you may have been encouraged and richly rewarded to move in the past, now it's viewed as a liability.

Rob's issue was a little more complicated. After several jumps, all short term and all easy to explain at the time, he was out of work for almost eight months. It was unbearable and in a moment of feeling vulnerable and restless, he decided to accept an offer to join a day trading firm. At least, he reasoned, it would allow him to keep his licenses and to sit for the Series 7. The firm promised to provide him with a platform to trade options. That never materialized, and he was forced to trade equities, a skill that he had never developed or had an interest in. He failed and left the firm with an accumulated loss of $50k.

Back in the job market, Rob networked his way into meetings with a top hedge fund. They "got" him and understood the reasons for the various moves. He had a series of good conversations and then—BAM—he was asked the question he was most terrified to answer:

What was your production? They wanted to know his numbers, all of them, at every firm where he had worked...not just as an options trader.

Rob called me immediately in a panic. He feared the worst, that the firm would reject him straight out, and that there would be no room or opportunity to explain. He thought that the six months at the day trading firm should have been omitted from the resume but that didn't address the issue at hand. He was asked to provide his numbers. It's easy under stress to exercise poor judgment and to blame yourself for events and outcomes that you may have been unable to control. In this case, Rob was kicking himself for having been honest on his resume. Honesty is never a bad thing. It just needs to be positioned correctly.

Regarding the creative omission issue, I'm a big advocate for "truth in advertising" when any or all of the following conditions exist:

- Not telling the truth will be discovered and damage your credibility.
- You have a FINRA U5 paper trail *and* you're interviewing with a firm that will perform a search.
- The truth is necessary and enhances your story.

In Rob's case, could he have kept secret his time at the day trading firm? Yes, but only if he was not planning to pursue another trading position. Rob's interests were better served by addressing the matter truthfully and on his own terms. This demonstrates that you're operating in good faith...and good conscience. After some deliberation, here's how he responded to the request:

> I'm happy to share my complete production history with you. It's pretty straightforward. I've had a great track record in trading options, and I was eager to get back to work...as I mentioned to you.
>
> I joined the firm with the goal of trading options—which they told me they did in addition to equities—so I was feeling pretty confident about the decision. When I started, I realized immediately that they really weren't committed to options. The focus was entirely short term.

I found myself trading equities, an area where I have virtually no interest or expertise. It was also at a particularly bad time in the market. You probably remember.

In truth, I didn't do well. I was down $50k when I made the decision to cut my losses. Trading equities: It's not what I like, and it's not what I want to do. Most important, I didn't want to damage my reputation any further.

Whenever you're faced with a situation like this—something bad that's happened but not something bad about you—the goal is to make an impression that's sincere and smart. Your explanation, like Rob's, should produce the following response from your audience: *I would have made that same decision, too.* If it makes sense and it's not overly complicated in telling, then you just may diffuse the problem as Rob did.

Why Did You Leave Your Job? Marilyn and Dan

Marilyn: Fired for Cause

This is often the most difficult separation to explain. How do you keep them interested in you after you've shared potentially damaging information? The challenge is to tell the truth but to do so in a way that keeps you as whole and as undamaged as possible. It's a tricky situation to navigate, and there is no guarantee that any strategy will work. Wall Street is not comfortable with problems, especially those that may not have been resolved neatly.

The first step is to determine how your former employer will present your separation to the world. You need to know what they're saying about you and your departure. Better to be aware of the very worst and use that as a reference point. On the other hand, it may be a non-event. Many companies are willing to say nothing rather than risk litigation. Next, outline the events as they really occurred, not as you would like to remember them. Then we construct a story—

entirely truthful—that positions you in as good a light as possible. In this particular case, we aim for good, not great.

Marilyn had inadvertently shared confidential information about a transaction with a friend. It was a harmless disclosure but she happened to mention it to her boss in passing. That led to an investigation by Human Resources. Marilyn admitted that she had experienced a lapse in judgment and without any ulterior motive. That was still considered grounds for immediate termination.

Marilyn was lucky. It so happened that the separation coincided with a downsizing, and her firm was willing to include her among the many employees being released as part of the RIF, a reduction in force. That meant that Marilyn would be eligible for a severance package based on her many years of service. If you've done something wrong, like Marilyn, you generally have no room to negotiate. It's really about relying on the kindness and compassion of your former colleagues. When they're calling the shots, you'll be lucky if you receive a severance package like Marilyn did. That's just the way the system works, even if what you did wrong seemed harmless at the time. On the other hand, it never hurts to ask.

Although she was upset and embarrassed by the decision, she was thrilled to receive a full year of severance, full medical benefits for the same period of time, and as icing on the cake, at least 26 weeks of unemployment insurance from the Department of Labor if she didn't find another job. Jackpot!

In truth, Marilyn had been unhappy at work for a long time. She began her career in the back office as an operations assistant. After 20 years and several promotions, she was responsible for a team of a dozen support specialists and managers. The idea of time off to contemplate the future was like winning the lottery. Having been separated in June, she decided that a summer break could be easily justified and was well-deserved. She had worked hard, and in the scheme of things, it seemed to be a small indulgence. It would also allow her some distance from a very painful divorce from her company. Besides 52 weeks was a very long time, and everyone knows, according to Marilyn, companies don't hire in the summer.

Well, summer led to a lovely fall, followed by a winter that was particularly cold and wet. Before she knew it, Marilyn's severance was about to run out. She had done little in the way of job search except to prepare her resume and infrequently surf the Internet and various job search websites. When we met, she was fearful and extremely anxious about finding a new position quickly. She was also willing to compromise on compensation, role, and scope of responsibility.

Here's my advice on taking time off. Do it if you want to and need to. Just know that you'll still have to conduct job search when you're ready to return to work. The market may have changed, and you'll have been out even longer. That means you'll need a good story to explain the time out, and there may be fewer opportunities available if the market has tanked. That's not a bad thing. It's just a fact that you have to take into account in making a decision about an extended break.

Regarding Marilyn, a sabbatical was a good thing. It gave her the time she desperately needed to decompress and to gain distance from a bad event. What she didn't plan for and should have was the eventual return to work. She also didn't use her time productively to explore alternative career options and themes. So, when the deadline for her severance was fast approaching, she shifted into default mode: a job like the one she had before. It was familiar, and she thought the search would be faster.

Marilyn, why did you leave your job?

We had a large downsizing at the firm. I suspected that something was up and, in truth, I'd been restless for a while. It's likely that folks knew about my desire to make a change and that may be how I found myself on the short list. I didn't ask. I was just so excited to be given this gift. At the time, I also knew that there were no other opportunities at the firm. We were in a hiring freeze.

Because Marilyn's separation was treated as a downsizing, she was under no obligation to explain the circumstances surrounding the event. It may come up, however, as you'll see here:

When did you leave?

If a career change is desired:

I left the firm about ten months ago. After 20 years there, I needed some time to clear my head and think about what I wanted to do in the next stage of my career. So I made the decision to take some time off.

I feel really fortunate that I was able to do this. First the summer and then to handle some family matters...aging parents, and so on. I've also been taking classes in a special certificate program for non-profit management at ABC University. My goal now is to find a position in fundraising and development.

If Marilyn is eager to get back to work and is willing to return to the kind of job she had before:

I left the firm about ten months ago. After 20 years there, I needed and wanted some time off. First the summer and then to handle some family matters...aging parents, and so on. I've also been attending various industry events and taking several classes to strengthen my skill set. I didn't have the time to do that sort of thing when I was working. So, I've officially been in job search for the last three months.

When explaining an extended period of time, it's not a bad idea to break down the time into discrete segments. In Marilyn's case, she has three distinct periods, as follows:

1. Summer.
2. Healthcare and continuing education.
3. Job search.

This technique makes it feel like Marilyn has not been in job search for that much time. That's a good impression. The longer you're out, the more questions are raised as to your value and desirability.

Who was your manager at the time?

Here's where Marilyn may find herself in slightly deeper water. If she provides the name of her manager, is it likely that a reference check would reveal what the downsizing hides? We'll cover references in another chapter, but for now, here's a suggested response:

I'd be happy to provide you with her name and contact information.

It's as simple as that. It's very likely that Marilyn's company has a policy on providing references, especially in the case of a large-scale downsizing. However, long before Marilyn interviews, she needs to have re-connected with her former boss to determine what, if anything, her boss will say about the separation. In this case, an extended time off has a benefit. It neutralizes much of the emotional turbulence and anger that may have existed early on. Her boss may be surprisingly supportive.

Dan: Choosing to Leave

Dan is a senior manager who made the difficult decision to leave his position at a mid-sized financial institution. It was his choice to go. Although he could have remained at the firm indefinitely, the environment and his role had changed dramatically. When there are no obvious issues or events like a downsizing or merger, it's a lot tougher to explain. You might also be viewed as either reckless or arrogant for appearing to make an impulsive decision. In a bear market, no one is inclined to believe you. And why should they? If you were on the other side of the table, how would you react? Yes, that's right...you must be hiding something.

Dan had a long and distinguished career at the firm. In his last two years there, he headed a large team of structured finance professionals engaged in transactions in the interest rate, municipal, and credit markets. For the ten years prior, he was the firm's head trader, and before that, he helped to establish its derivatives platform. The bank brought in a well-known consulting firm to evaluate its capital markets division, and several months and several million dollars later, the business was ripped apart and re-constructed. In addition to the structural changes, many of Dan's long-time colleagues were released. It was a solitary new world for him. He felt that the new strategy was destined to fail, and he wasn't willing to be taken down, too.

Dan had several conversations with top management regarding his concerns. At the end of the day, it didn't make a difference. He wasn't confident in the direction the bank was headed in and they were unwilling to address his concerns. He wasn't fired. There was no severance to negotiate. The bank would have preferred that he stay. All things considered, it was an amicable, albeit unprofitable, divorce.

Dan took a few months off to get his life back in order and to spend a good chunk of time with his family. He was referred to me by a former client of mine and a former colleague of his. He left a voice-mail message for me about needing to get back to work but not ever having done a job search. He had already begun to test the water and discovered that it was far colder than he imagined. He was scared, and he was also feeling like he wasn't presenting himself in the very best possible light. In a recent interview, he was grilled on the decision to leave his firm. It didn't go well—he knew it—and he was eliminated in the first round. Yikes! Not many opportunities out there, and he blew a good one.

Here's what we came up with to explain the separation:

I can't go into a lot of detail regarding the decision to leave. [This implies that you signed a non-disclosure agreement, which means you cannot and will not disparage the firm. By inference, to be critical would convey poor judgment. It doesn't matter if you actually signed an agreement; it's the impression that you may have and, if so, that you're exercising good and very desirable judgment.] However, it might be helpful to give you a little background on various events and what was happening at the time.

Briefly, the group was relocated back to New York from Greenwich:

- The business was in the process of being broken up and broken down. All of the business units were being transferred to other areas.

- There was a mass exodus out of the firm. Lots of folks were leaving.

- A major change was also introduced in the way we were being compensated. We moved from a formula that was tied directly to performance to a completely subjective basis. That decision felt heavy handed and unfair.

My contract expired. I'd been there for 18 years, and I was prepared and ready to graduate. You're probably thinking: How could he have made that decision at such a horrible time in the economy? I was also asked to take on an additional role managing a business that was under IRS, DOJ, and SEC investigation. Given everything else that had happened and my need for a change, I wasn't willing to expose myself to the potential reputational fallout.

Why did he leave? In Dan's case, the message had to be that he was in the driver's seat, not the firm. He was responsible for making the decision and for any and all of the consequences that would arise. A choice to leave voluntarily is often met with skepticism, especially in a market where new opportunities are few and far between. It was critical for Dan to convey confidence tempered by good judgment.

Anything less or different would have been viewed as foolhardy. You, like Dan, need to have an underlying theme that propels the explanation. For Dan, his old firm no longer offered him the platform he needed to continue to achieve the kind of success he had in the past.

Ann: Explaining an Awkward and Potentially Embarrassing Event

Sometimes an event will occur that has the potential to diminish your attractiveness. It's possible that it may have been avoided if you worked harder or exercised better judgment. It's also possible that it may have happened anyway. There is no way to know whether working harder or establishing the right relationships would have made a difference. What *do* you know? First, that you will not make the same mistake again. Second, that you will need a convincing, legitimate explanation which preserves and maintains your equity as a candidate. Please don't obsess over what has already happened. It's over. Just commit to understanding what happened and why. Then take time to strategize on how to best present.

When Ann started business school, it became immediately clear that the job market would be tough and few opportunities would be available. Companies that were usually big consumers of MBA talent eliminated their recruiting schedules both for summer and full-time positions. Despite great experience with a large investment manager before B-school, she was presented with few options as a summer associate and then just one as a second year student.

The foreign bank that hired her for the summer and subsequently offered her a permanent position was her only option. Ann joined the bank and then six months later, it was merged with another institution. She lost her job in a large downsizing that was unavoidable. It was devastating to her ego, yes, and terrifying to her financial security. She gave serious thought to a return home to southern California.

Although there were fewer opportunities available there, she could use her parents' home as a base to conduct her job search.

Maybe she just wasn't cut out for the intense pressure of a high-powered career on Wall Street. Coincidentally, her lease was about to expire on her apartment. It seemed like the right decision. At the moment she was about to pull the trigger and arrange for the moving company to pack up her stuff, she received a call from a large hedge fund for a junior portfolio manager position. They saw her resume on the internet and wanted to meet with her. It's amazing how a single call can make all the difference in the world.

Fast forward two weeks. Ann e-mailed me in a panic. Not because the interview with the hedge fund went poorly...just the opposite. It went extremely well, and she was invited back for additional meetings. It was August, and she just received the results from level three of the CFA exam, which she had taken in June. She failed by a nose. She had just interviewed with the hedge fund the week before. The firm had her old resume, which indicated that she would be sitting for level three, and it had also come up in her meetings. How to handle this potentially damaging development?

Ann initially wanted to come clean, spill her guts, and tell everyone about the failure. She also toyed with the idea of submitting a newly revised resume with level three omitted. Neither seemed like the right option to me. I do believe in "truth in advertising" at every point in the interviewing process. Anything less than complete honesty—with artful editing—will get you into trouble. Yes, she should own up to her CFA status, but only when the question was raised. It was possible that no one would even ask. With respect to her resume, presenting a modified document after the first set of meetings seemed awfully suspicious.

In any difficult situation, it's always a good idea to take a step and a moment back to gain perspective. Was failing level three of the CFA exam a monumental issue? No! Lots of smart people fail. As I pointed out to Ann, only one of her five interviewers had the designation. It's very likely any one of them could have failed a level or two or decided not to even pursue the designation. In preparing for the first round of interviews at the firm, Ann was introduced to another woman from her business school who worked there. She was extremely helpful in providing background on the people Ann would be meeting with, the culture of the firm, and attributes and skills to emphasize. We decided that Ann should turn to this woman again to get her advice on how to handle this situation. She was helpful and discreet the first time around. It seemed like an obvious step to take to turn to an "insider:"

> Thanks so much for chatting with me. You were so incredibly helpful when I was preparing for my first round of meetings. As I mentioned to you in my e-mail, it all went really well, and I've been invited back. I'm deeply grateful to you.
>
> I was hoping to get your advice as I prepare for the next round of meetings. I also wanted to see how you think I should handle a potentially awkward situation...off the record.
>
> I took level three of the CFA exam and just found out that I didn't pass [notice here that Ann does not use the word "fail"]. I feel so angry at myself. I wanted to get your advice on how to handle it if the question comes up in the interview. If it's helpful to know, I was in the top ten decile of non-passers. It's small comfort, but it is what it is. I intend to take level three again, and I'll do so next year.

The woman, like me, didn't think it was a big deal. She also advised Ann on not introducing the matter unless she was asked directly. If Ann was asked, her contact advised her to own up to this new development but never apologize. Ann should frame her response thus:

> Since my interviews last week, I was notified that I didn't pass level three. Naturally, I was disappointed. It was a genuinely humbling experience. Although I scored in the top ten decile of non-passers, I could have and should have passed. I even know the three questions that I blew. Next year, that won't happen.

Never belabor the matter. Just express your disappointment and convey the knowledge that you've gained as a result of this experience. Thoughtfulness and reflection go a long way in defusing a potentially awkward or embarrassing situation.

Questions to Ask

The best interviews feel like a love fest. They're conversations where the information flows effortlessly. It's as if you've known each other forever. Call it déjà vu. It all happens naturally, energetically, and with a sense of purpose. Your interviewer asks you questions, you feel good about how you respond, and you're equally engaged asking questions. You're on, and everyone is smiling.

That's interviewing at its best. If only. Unfortunately, it generally doesn't unfold that way. That's why preparation and practice are essential to success. So far, we've considered one side of the interview equation: what you may be asked under a variety of scenarios, some obvious and others less so. You've been advised on how to prepare for more challenging situations. You've also been given examples of real clients who were not initially effective in dealing with these situations. We've yet to consider the questions you'll be expected to ask. They have the power to make or break you.

No matter how tough your interviewer may be, a successful interview is not measured only by how you respond to questions. It's a performance, yes, but a good interview involves audience participation. It's interactive and informational. Naturally, you need to show that you're comfortable and knowledgeable. You also need to convey that you've done your homework. You cannot afford to let the ball slip. You have far too much riding on the success of your interview to wing it, even when it comes to the questions you ask.

Always—ALWAYS—be prepared to ask questions in an interview. You have no excuse at this point in the process to think that your questions are less important than any of the other information you share about yourself. The point is to demonstrate that you have a genuine interest in both the job and the organization—even if you don't. It's the driver's seat strategy I mentioned earlier. That's where you want to be when a decision is made about you as a candidate.

Generally, the interview questions you ask should reflect the in-depth research you've gathered throughout the interview process. Your knowledge of the organization and its challenges should define the direction your questions take. One more point, and it's an important one: It doesn't matter how your interviewer treats you. Unless you've been hit or insulted—in that case, call your lawyer and local law enforcement immediately—your tone must never be adversarial. It may just be a test. If it's not, then there's no need to stoop to a level that compromises your integrity or dignity.

It's impossible for me to predict what approach to take with respect to the questions you ask. I don't presume to know which questions will work in any specific situation. What I do know is that a couple of very obvious questions will keep the conversation moving forward and impress your interviewer. These are what I refer to as the "money" questions. They're not intended to replace the kinds of questions that should arise naturally in the course of a conversation. But they are guaranteed to make you look and sound smart.

These are my top five. I'm sure there are many, many more:

1. **What is the most important contribution I can make in my first six months?**

   Picture this: You're interviewing yourself. What would you like to hear? Wouldn't you want to know what you as a candidate could do to make a difference? What solutions will you introduce that have the potential to add real, meaningful value within a reasonable timeframe? Six months seems fair. Much shorter, and there's no guarantee that you'll have the time to complete an ambitious project. Longer than that, and there's the potential to get distracted or forget why it was important in the first place.

Notice that I've also personalized this question by using the word "my." Of course, you're not working there yet, but the "my" suggests that you'd like to. It's not presumptuous. It sounds like you've already made a commitment.

Here's a variation on the first question with a slight twist: How will you measure my success? In the first version, the focus is on what needs to be fixed. Now you and they are looking back and asking whether you've accomplished what they wanted you to and how that will be determined. You expect to be productive, and you want them to be clear on your commitment and confidence.

2. **If there's been turnover in the position that hasn't been explained: Can you tell me about the history of this position? How long has it been open?**

   What are you getting yourself into? If there's been a long list of people who were not successful in this position, what makes you think you'll be any different? On the other hand, there may be a legitimate story that provides reasonable and reassuring context. At the end of the day, if you need a job and there are no others in sight, of course you do what you have to—accept a job that may not work out. But don't ignore the red flags going in. Just know that the potential exists for the bottom to fall out, don't kick yourself if it does, and prepare for a bumpy landing.

3. **If the position is brand new, ask why: What led to the creation of this position?**

   Knowledge is power. Understanding why the position was considered important enough to establish—and it takes a lot to get one approved in a challenging market—gives you some insight into how and why decisions are made. It also offers you a perspective on how you can add value both now and over the longer term. Don't hesitate to share your unique qualifications and experience.

On the other hand, it's possible that this may be a "vanity" position—one that was created impulsively or based upon an unsupportable platform. Without a reason for a job to exist, you could find yourself in a very vulnerable spot should cuts happen, your boss leaves, or there's a reorganization. Does this position exist elsewhere in the company? If yes, you may be stepping into a political minefield. Being new, you'll be unfamiliar with the resources that are critical to ensure your success. You also won't have a rabbi to point you in the right direction or protect you.

4. What are the ideal qualifications in a great candidate?

I'd want to know what qualities are viewed as attractive by the person you'll be working for and by the organization. Having this information as a benchmark serves several purposes. First, it allows you to highlight those qualities and qualifications you possess that will position you in the very best possible light. Having this information also points out potential gaps. The challenge, then, is either to minimize the downside of not being a "10" or promote other strengths to offset or neutralize your deficits.

5. Tell me about your management style and how you generally work with the people who report to you.

Are your work styles in sync? What's that about the devil you know? If you have any doubts about the person you'll be working for, better to know what you're getting yourself into. This question also allows you to showcase specific qualities and talents that may be attractive to your interviewer. For example, if he or she has a "hands-off" management style, then you should find a way to illustrate your capacity to work both independently and successfully.

In asking the interviewer questions, please try to minimize the "me" factor. That's when the questions you ask focus primarily on you and how you stand to benefit. When you interview, save the self-serving agenda and self-promotion for the very tail-end. By that point, which I'm expecting you will and should reach, you'll be closer to negotiating both the role and the terms of an offer. So yes, by then, asking about vacation days will be a legitimate question. For the time being, think about what information you and the interviewer will need to share to get you closer to a favorable decision.

8

Write On: Effective Career Correspondence

Managing your job search is essentially about developing a communications strategy. You use a resume to capture the key themes that define your career. You practice interviewing to ensure that you present your qualifications and knowledge in a way that distinguishes you from other candidates. You correspond to establish and nurture relationships. There are a number of moving parts, and it may sometimes feel like you're cajoling a herd of elephants up a hill. Collectively, it's a time-consuming, labor-intensive process. That's why you need a few shortcuts to speed you along.

Correspondence is often the missing link between success and failure in job search. Let's refer to it as "failure to follow up." You've done everything right: networked your way into the company, generated interest in your qualifications, and begun to interview. Then the breakdown happens. You forget to prepare a thoughtful, substantive follow-up or you're delinquent. It doesn't matter. Both are bad and diminish you as a candidate.

There is no debate. When you interview, you must always follow up. It doesn't matter what your level is in the organizational food chain, and it doesn't make a difference what the timeframe is for turnaround (because the time they tell you they'll have a decision is never based in reality). The people you meet like to know that you, first and foremost, benefited from the conversation, and if it's an official interview, that you left with a greater appreciation of the position, its importance to the organization, and the potential for you to add value. If it's a networking meeting, it's all about knowledge gained and engaging in some over-the-top gushing to show that you're grateful. That's one step beyond thanks.

If you've lost interest in the job, then you disengage responsibly. You never know how and when your past will resurface in job search. Sending a note is a small price to pay to maintain a positive image and an unblemished reputation. If you suspect they've lost interest in you, please be careful not to jump to a hasty conclusion. I've had many clients who misread the signals. They've taken silence as a lack of interest when, in fact, the process just stalled due to other more important events. Imagine losing out on an opportunity when you actually made a great impression and just neglected to follow up. That happens.

When the competition is intense, you distinguish yourself from other candidates through the quality of your follow-up. What you say after a meeting must always emphasize five key points, as follows:

1. **Gratitude.** Their time is valuable and that needs to be recognized.

2. **An understanding of the position if you've interviewed for one, or the subject matter discussed if it's a networking meeting.** They need to know that you're worthy of their time. They also need to feel and see your passion and enthusiasm.

3. **What you offer as an employee that qualifies you above the competition, and distinguishes you from everyone else.** There are lots of people with whom they can spend their time. Why you?

4. **How they will benefit.** Managers are overwhelmed at every level in the organization. What have you taken away from the meeting that you can begin to translate into a solution for them?

5. **Next steps.** What are their intentions and how should you proceed? You're not being overly forceful. You're gaining clarification and you're also determining how to support them in making the very best possible decision.

Types of Correspondence

Every word counts in your correspondence. Always know what you want to say and why it needs to be said. Then think about how. I've described previously why good follow-up is important. That represents only one segment of your job search. Look at the search as a timeline. It begins with how you get introduced, and tracks your job search all the way through to what you write to convey that you're the best candidate after many rounds of interviews. The types of job search correspondence are varied and generally fall within one of the following five categories:

1. **Responding to online and other job postings.** This is a boilerplate e-mail or, alternatively, a "cut and paste" of your resume for an online application. Please don't obsess over content. Instead, provide a data dump of all the relevant information that will support you as a candidate. If your resume and letter are scanned virtually, then you want to make sure you're covering every possible angle. You don't want to spend hours preparing a response when the odds of hearing back are not in your favor. On the other hand, your correspondence needs to be both readable and smart.

   Don't experiment with alternative formats. When jobs are posted, the expectation is a traditional response that will be easily processed and presented to the reader. This is not a vehicle to use to try and draw attention to yourself especially if you believe you're the right candidate. If you have access to the name of the company, this is where you find a way to distinguish yourself. How about the timing of your response?

Immediate or wait? It doesn't matter. It's the content that will make you stand out.

As a rule, you use one of two letters. Both letters begin with an explanation as to why you're writing: *I'm responding to your posting for....* The second paragraph highlights your background: *My background, briefly....* The third paragraph is where the letters diverge. Remember the folded paper exercise in Chapter 1, "The Wall Street Job Search: Winning in Any Market"? On one side, you listed options, and on the other side, you listed your qualifications. The first version is a variation on that theme. You list the key requirements for the job in the left column—desired skills, experience, and other attributes—and in the right column, you match up your qualifications with each bullet.

Alternatively, if you fall short on any of the qualifications, there's no need to draw further attention to the deficit. The approach described previously works best when you can check off all the boxes. If you're a great candidate but not perfect, use the third paragraph to highlight a couple of your accomplishments using bullets. These accomplishments should be tied directly to the core requirements of the job and demonstrate your ability to be effective, productive, and valuable immediately.

2. **Networking letters and notes.** This is the "reaching out" category. Here your goal is to find the best balance between pest and forgettable. It is, in fact, a continuum. Sometimes you'll end up on the wrong end. So be it. The goal in networking is to establish a relationship, which means that the person you write to needs a reason to want to get to know you. If they don't know you, they have every reason to be protective of their time. You also need to be absolutely clear that you're not writing to them for a job. That's not networking. It's a burden that you're dumping into their lap. You'll read about Eric in a moment and see two examples of networking correspondence.

Networking should also include a strategy for tapping into social media options such as LinkedIn, Facebook, and Twitter, just three of many sites. The potential to mine these communities is infinite. Generally, the people who participate are already networking-minded. That's why they're there. When you reach out to them, there's a good chance they'll respond. Put yourself on their end of the e-mail exchange. Why would you be willing to meet with yourself? You'll need a good reason, and it can't be just to pick their brain. If that's the case, they're going to see the conversation with you—a complete stranger or even a long lost friend—to be entirely one-sided and weighted to benefit you. Not much of an incentive to make themselves available!

3. **Direct mail.** In job search, you expand your reach by contacting companies directly. This is similar to the kind of letter you receive from a bank marketing its credit cards or the phone company selling a new service. You may throw out the letter, but some people don't. Even if the response rate is low, say 1 or 2%, it's still significant. If you can personalize the letter to make it feel like it's been e-mailed to one company, not dozens, the rate is higher.

Direct mail is one step in a comprehensive job search campaign. Because its success rate is low, please don't spend more time on this category than it deserves. Think about it as your "return on job search investment." Are you getting back what you're putting in? Probably not, but once you've created the boilerplate, see if it works. If you've established reasonable expectations and the letter produces a response, it's good to go. You can use it as a boilerplate for other mailings.

I use the word "letter" throughout. What I really mean is e-mail. That's the prevailing mode of correspondence. Clients will sometimes say that a hard copy letter will stand out. Yes, it will, but probably for the wrong reasons. It will make you look like a dinosaur. Everyone uses e-mail. The exceptions: If you know your correspondence will end up as spam, then of course, you have no choice but to send a hard copy. The same goes if you've exhausted every option to find an e-mail address.

4. **Follow-ups to meetings.** I've already devoted enough air space to follow-up correspondence. This is the "make or break" category. Every meeting gets your time and attention, some more so than others. You must always follow up! Enough said.

5. **An analysis.** At some point in the interviewing process, you may find that the role you are being considered for or the organization where you will work has some issue or challenge that will require intervention. That's a desirable development because it gives you a reason to distinguish yourself from other candidates. Your follow-up should focus on solutions and strategy. It will be based on the information you've gathered from many conversations and from your prior experience. This form of correspondence looks more like an analysis combined with recommendations.

Companies want to know that you can be an impact player on day one, and that you're clear on what needs to happen to be productive immediately. That's why Wall Street and other financial services firms will often pay a premium for talent. There's no tolerance for long lead times or coming up to speed. The mood is driven by a sense of urgency and the fear of competition. If a problem exists, they want to know how you'll fix it. It's the short attention span approach to management: Get it done now.

This is where you may face a dilemma, where the potential exists for crossing over from enthusiasm to fiction. They may want to hear something to convince them that you're the right candidate and that something may be impossible to accomplish. Your goal is to convey your passion, excitement, and knowledge. It's also to demonstrate how you'll mobilize these resources to achieve realistic expectations. Passion goes a long way in mitigating unrealistic hopes and beliefs. Just make sure you don't over-compensate. If their expectations are not aligned with yours, it's likely you'll find yourself back in job search before you're ready.

Eric, Age 38: Intern and Incredible Networker

This next illustration is one of my favorites. It's a hybrid in terms of career themes and strategy and has the potential to describe best practices on a range of career matters. Because of its versatility, it could have been presented in several of the chapters. It's about assessment, strategy, correspondence, interviewing, and negotiation. Mostly, though, it describes a very thoughtful and courageous fellow, Eric, who decided to change the course of his life and career at the age of 38. He invested a lot of time, energy, and attention in deciding on the direction to pursue, and he was also tireless in practicing to make the most of his interviews. But the real turning point for Eric was tied directly to his correspondence. It was sincere and focused, and presented simply and logically what he wanted and why. It also worked.

Not long ago, I met Eric at a lecture I had given to a local chapter of the CFA Institute. He introduced himself after the Q&A and explained that he wanted to move from risk management to fee-based financial planning. He was part of a large downsizing at a major financial institution where he and his team oversaw a portfolio of commercial and residential mortgage-backed securities, asset-backed securities, and collateralized debt obligations. Eric enjoyed his role as an advisor to the bank's internal clients, and he liked the technical nature of his subject matter. The feedback was consistently positive, too. He had begun the CFA process several years before but realized early on that his interests were individually, not institutionally, based. He had passed level one and then put preparation for level two on a permanent hiatus. A few years later, he re-visited certifications and discovered the Certified Financial Planner (CFP) designation, which he began to prepare for immediately. He'd found his target. It was perfect for him. At the time that Eric had introduced himself to me, he had just completed a course of study and he was about to sit for the certification exam.

As Eric began to research the fee-based financial planning community, he discovered that the majority of firms were small, generally with ten employees or fewer. Although he didn't have a clear strategy in mind, this direction felt right...so the big question for him was where to begin? Through his research, Eric found several sources of information, some of which he discovered in obvious but unlikely places. In fact, he hit the mother lode: a comprehensive list including names of principals and their contact information in a major consumer publication. He used that as a basis to begin his job search. He also joined every organization in the field that held meetings and conferences.

For Eric, the initial steps were the most important. I knew that once he gained some traction, the people he met with would see him as passionate, smart, and committed to pursuing this new direction. What follows are two examples of Eric's networking correspondence. These are the letters that propelled his search. Once he got going, he was intrepid. Eric also knew that writing good letters would discipline him to establish the same standards for his other correspondence at every step of the search. Why have I referred to him as an intern? That's because he ultimately used an unpaid internship as the springboard to re-direct his career.

Eric's First Networking Letter

Dear (FIRST NAME),

It was great to see you at the (EVENT). As you may recall, we also met previously at (ANOTHER EVENT). I was glad that (NAME OF PERSON) re-introduced us.

Let me explain my reason for contacting you. I recently left (NAME OF COMPANY), and I am in the process of gathering ideas and information as I move forward in my career. My goal, as you may recall, is to eventually move to a financial planning firm.

In my role as a (YOUR JOB) at (NAME OF COMPANY), I was a member of a diverse team responsible for building a (THE FUNCTIONAL DISCIPLINE; FOR EXAMPLE, RISK MANAGEMENT METHODOLOGY). My principal focus was on identifying risk exposure in (NAME OF COMPANY)'s portfolio of structured securities, and as I am sure you can appreciate, much of my time was devoted to CMBS in recent months.

My intention for the time being is solely to meet colleagues in the financial planning industry and to expand my network. (WHERE THE PERSON YOU'RE WRITING TO WORKS) is at the center of many exciting ventures and would be a wonderful resource for me to make contact. To facilitate our conversation, I am attaching my resume to provide some additional background.

Thank you for taking a moment to read my e-mail. These are very exciting times for (WHERE THE PERSON YOU'RE WRITING TO WORKS). Based upon the cutting-edge initiatives you're spearheading, it would be immensely valuable to gain your insight and perspective. I look forward to our conversation and will follow up with you over the next couple of days.

Best regards,

Eric's Second Networking Letter: A Slightly More Complicated Story to Tell

Dear (FIRST NAME),

I believe you may have received my name and correspondence from (NAME OF PERSON A). I was introduced to him by (PERSON B). As (PERSON A) may have indicated to you, I am deeply committed to making the move from a corporate risk management role to financial planning, and both (PERSON A and PERSON B) felt that your advice would be invaluable.

My background, briefly: Until recently, I was with (NAME OF COMPANY) in credit risk management where I (DESCRIBE RESPONSIBILITIES). My qualifications include expertise in analyzing financial information, translating complex topics for a range of constituents, and an ability to plan, organize, and execute important projects. Above and beyond all else, I have acquired a deep appreciation for the need to maintain the absolutely highest standards of integrity, loyalty, and trust.

In addition to a BS in business from (NAME OF SCHOOL), I recently was awarded the CFP designation. I'm ready now to move forward!

It would be a great honor to meet with you in person, even if you have only a few minutes to spare. I know and expect that your time is valuable. When I do call to follow up, I promise to be brief. Thank you in advance.

Sincerely,

Tom: Moving from the Sell-Side to the Buy-Side

Here's an example of a letter that combines networking with a desire to propel job search. Tom was a trader for many years. His letter may seem redundant and a little dense. That's the point. He's a smart, analytical fellow. He wanted to create the impression that he wasn't the stereotypical "ADD" type trader. He also wanted to use a lot of language that would emphasize his depth of knowledge across many categories of fixed income and his ability to perform detailed, rigorous analysis:

Dear (FIRST OR LAST NAME),

I met with (NAME OF CONTACT) recently, and he suggested that I send you a copy of my resume. After my conversation with (FIRST NAME OF THE SAME CONTACT), I am very interested in (NAME OF BANK)'s Corporate Research and Asset Management

Division because of your specialized analysis of the credit markets and the smaller boutique-style environment. I have a breadth of experience in sectors that your group focuses on, and therefore, I believe that my background and professional interests may be well-suited to (NAME OF BANK OR ITS ACRONYM).

My goal is to move from the sell-side to the buy-side, and I am committed to making this transition successfully. I am equally committed to being a positive contributor to a portfolio management team. Throughout my career, I have consistently taken a more analytically oriented approach to my work as a trader by incorporating research and relative value trading to my daily trading responsibilities. After many conversations and much research, it has become increasingly clear to me that portfolio management is the right direction to pursue. Throughout my ten years of trading, I have become increasingly interested in not only the buy-side, but more specifically portfolio management, and by taking the CFA exam, it further developed my understanding and knowledge of the investment side of the business. With this goal in mind, I was awarded the CFA designation after passing three consecutive exams while working full-time.

My background, briefly: I am currently a trader with (NAME OF BANK) with a focus on trading (CATEGORIES), as well as trading with all the firm's institutional accounts looking to transact in smaller size trades—$3mm and under. I have traded across most fixed income credit markets and sectors including emerging markets, high yield, distressed, and most of the investment grade sectors—that is, (LIST THEM). As a result of this combined experience, I am very comfortable transacting, positioning, and analyzing bonds in almost all the credit markets, and I also have a good working knowledge of the credit default swaps and leveraged loan markets. Additionally, I have consistently increased trading volumes and P&L on average at least 10% year over year.

Thank you for taking the time to read this note. I have attached my resume, which provides additional background information.

I look forward to having the opportunity to meet with you. I will follow up with a call in a few days.

Sincerely,

Dave: Career Change Networking Letter

Dave was at the beginning of his job search. It was the point where he still needed to confirm that he was on the right track but ready to take the conversations one step beyond information gathering. He was clear on his target. Now he was test driving the proposition.

In his e-mail, Dave wanted to demonstrate his passion for making the change, that he was absolutely clear on why, and that he knew that he was well qualified to do so. The correspondence was part tap dance routine and part request. He needed to impress the reader enough to get them to agree to spend time with him and to share both their knowledge and contacts. The e-mail was sent selectively, and it generated an almost 100% positive response rate. Notice how Dave also takes initiative for following up. You have to do so, too:

Dear (NAME),

After significant success as a sell-side and buy-side equity analyst, I am now committed to pursuing a career in investor relations and strategic communications. At this point in the process, my goal is to meet with prominent leaders in the field so that I can increase my knowledge and understanding of investor relations consulting and help better position myself for this move. I would greatly appreciate just a bit of your time to meet with you and discuss your field.

My industry experience has focused primarily around (INDUSTRY A) and (INDUSTRY B). In addition, I have an MBA from (NAME OF SCHOOL) and a Ph.D. in (SUBJECT) from (NAME OF SCHOOL). My qualifications include expertise in analyzing financial statements and building financial forecasts, translating complex topics for general audiences and transmitting the information in a timely and concise manner, and an ability to plan, organize, and execute complicated projects. Most importantly, I have acquired a deep understanding of what analysts and investors require and value from corporate communications.

I also believe that these skills are highly transferable and valuable to investor relations. I have also become an active member of (NAME OF PROFESSIONAL ORGANIZATION), which I have found to be valuable for learning about aspects of investor relations that one in equity research is not normally exposed to.

Thank you in advance for your consideration. I will call in a few days to follow up with you if only to get recommendations on people and firms to get to know. In the meantime, I can be reached at (PHONE #) or (E-MAIL).

Sincerely,

Nina: Direct Mail

Nina is a senior business developer. She's been around awhile, and that's why her letter focuses on revenue, production, and relationships. Remember, there's a low response rate for this category. Most readers of direct mail, if your correspondence *is* read, are looking for what you bring to the table right now: *Is it worth my time to meet you?* Nina also wanted to downplay and neutralize her age by presenting other numbers that would be more powerful. Most important, the message needed to be immediate.

Dear (FIRST NAME),

Since (NAME OF BANK) is a leader in private wealth management, I believe my enclosed resume may be of interest to you.

As a senior business development professional, I have successfully cultivated key relationships with high net worth and ultra high net worth individuals, corporate executives, and philanthropic institutions. Many of these clients are, if not household names, substantial in terms of their assets. These activities have produced double-digit annual growth in revenue, consistently and with increasing magnitude. My private banking career was highlighted by my position as a senior vice president and business development officer for (NAME OF BANK) with leadership responsibility for developing new clients and referral sources.

In becoming a financial advisor first at (NAME OF SECURITIES FIRM) and more recently at (NAME OF SECOND SECURITIES FIRM), I have increased my database to more than 1,200 personal contacts and have established real traction with a number of prospective high net worth clients. Currently, I am also developing significant global business opportunities, which I would like to discuss in greater detail with you.

I welcome the opportunity to speak with you about positions that may be available and will call you next week to request a meeting.

Thank you for your consideration.

Sincerely,

Jane: Recruiter Letter

There are two types of correspondence to recruiters. One is a general broadcast letter, and the other a response to a posting or to information you may have heard about an assignment. Except for the opening paragraph, they're the same letter. Recruiters generally ignore the correspondence and go straight to the resume. Nevertheless, it's customary to have a letter to provide context, and that doesn't mean you should let your standards slide. Although it will most likely not be read, your resume alone would make the wrong impression.

For the exception, however, where a recruiter shows a more active interest, please make sure to write a letter that gets to the point clearly and efficiently and positions you attractively. The information you provide needs to be logical and it has to flow. You don't need a great letter, just one that's adequate. That's why I'm providing this boilerplate. It works, and it's simple. Here's the format:

1. First paragraph: How you heard about the position or simply presenting yourself as a candidate for an assignment.
2. Second paragraph: Your background...briefly.
3. Third optional paragraph: A few key highlights either in paragraph form or bullets.
4. Fourth paragraph: The close. If you can follow up, or plan to, say that you will.

Dear (NAME OF RECRUITER),

In the event you are recruiting candidates for (TYPE OR TYPES OF POSITION; FOR EXAMPLE, SENIOR OPERATIONS/COO/CAO POSITIONS) where a legal background would be helpful, please take a moment to review the attached resume.

My background, briefly....

I would be delighted to speak with you about my experience, interests, and qualifications in greater detail. Additionally, should you be seeking candidates with backgrounds different from mine, I would be happy to share my resources and open my rolodex.

I will follow up by (DATE) to chat briefly and to make sure you have received this correspondence. In the meantime, I can also be reached at either (NUMBER) or (E-MAIL).

Sincerely,

Arthur: Social Networking Note

Social networking sites are invaluable for building and expanding your network. You know this, and you may already be "Tweeting." It's immediate and available. It's a network in a box. Here's the strategy. Follow the steps. The sample is Arthur's, and it worked for him:

1. Send a note to reach out. If you ask outright in the note for help, it's likely you won't hear back...unless you're sending it to your mother.

2. The burden is yours to make sure it's been received.

3. You arrange to meet and speak.

4. The request is made for assistance. Hopefully, you won't need to ask for what you want. It will be forthcoming, and the person you've arranged to meet will volunteer their help, support, and advice. If not, just ask.

Dear (NAME),

Paragraph 1: It's been a long time since we were last in touch, far too long. I'm not great at keeping up with friends. But now that I've recently left (YOUR JOB AND COMPANY NAME), I have a little extra time, and it's been great to see what my friends are doing. I'd love to hear about developments in your life and career.

Paragraph 2: Share some of your recent background, both professional and personal, if appropriate.

Paragraph 3: Explain how you'll follow up.

Bob: A Short Thank You

It's a "gusher." It's effusive but appropriate for a senior executive like Bob. He's combined gratitude with an understanding of the issues and challenges the bank is facing. He's also offering some insight into his potential to add value *and* he's extending his network and support unconditionally. It covers a lot in just a few short paragraphs.

Dear (NAME),

Thank you for taking time out of your busy schedule to meet last week and for arranging my conversation with (NAME #2). What an interesting and exciting time for you and (NAME OF BANK)—many important changes and much growth under way.

As you highlighted in our conversation, the focus now is on driving and sustaining the growth strategy that is already in place. Clearly, funding, liquidity, and risk management are dynamic, ongoing issues that will require increasing attention and creativity as the business expands.

I have given considerable thought to our conversation, and I am genuinely intrigued and interested. Equally important, from your perspective, I am confident that my experience would accelerate and enhance your goals. Your challenges are similar to those I faced and successfully addressed at (FORMER EMPLOYER). I was critically involved in supporting the growth of key businesses while managing their impact on capital, risk, and profitability.

Additionally, the timing of our meeting feels right. I am ready to take on new challenges, especially in an environment that is dynamic and growth oriented. I can offer (NAME OF BANK) extensive background in (FUNCTIONAL AREAS), and I know that I will add value immediately.

I look forward to continuing our conversation. In the meantime, if I can be of any help to you, please don't hesitate to contact me.

Regards,

Linda: How to Begin a Letter to a Hiring Manager When You Know There's an Opening

Sometimes clients get stumped by the obvious. In Linda's case, it was figuring out how to explain the reason for the introduction. I asked her how she heard about the potential opportunity and wrote word for word almost everything she told me. Do the same. Also, learn how to use the recording feature on your PDA if you have one or purchase a small handheld recorder. It will save you a lot of time trying to re-construct what may have sounded brilliant at the time:

> I've heard through several colleagues in the industry that the position as (JOB TITLE) reporting to you may be available.

In the event that this information is correct, I would like to ensure that you know of my background, qualifications, and interest. A resume and transaction list are attached.

Summary

This chapter on correspondence was not intended to be comprehensive. The goal is to offer you food for thought. I'm sure you've realized that much of the focus has been placed on networking. That's for several reasons, as follows:

1. Most people are reluctant to network, despite knowing that most successful job search begins here.

2. The correspondence doesn't need to be elaborate, just compelling.

3. Seeing examples of notes that have worked makes it abundantly clear that you don't have to devote a lot of time to this process...as long as you follow the steps.

The examples here have been stripped down to show construction versus content. By all means, borrow the letters for your own use. But please make sure to personalize them. If the letters do get read, you need to use language that's all yours...not mine.

9

Win-Win Negotiating in Job Search

When it comes to your career, negotiating with your employer generally occurs at two critical turning points: going in and exiting. Upon entry and long before you find yourself with an offer, how do you make sure that you receive the very best and most favorable terms in this challenging market? The inverse: In departing, how do you ensure that you get the most from the divorce, especially when the separation is more than likely to be involuntary? Both are equally important activities and should be viewed as a seamless process, part of the same continuum with job search on one end and managing your "life at work" on the other. That's how negotiating works in career management.

If you've negotiated successfully and thoughtfully upon entry, then much of what you should expect upon leaving will have already been determined. It's not a guarantee, however, in a market where the rules are changing moment to moment. Of course, if you're managing a dynamic career, you're one of the very few, unlike the rest of us, who's negotiating every step of the way. Matters like promotions, reviews, raises, bonuses, and political issues will inevitably arise, as will opportunities for mobility. That's a topic for another chapter. Right now, let's consider the basics: what to do when you're interviewing and get an offer...and what to do when you get fired.

I've found over time that it's a lot easier to advise others on best practices and approaches. So yes, being a critic has its advantages. I know that negotiation doesn't come easy for many of us, and I include myself among the "negotiation challenged." Fortunately, I've worked with thousands of clients on negotiating strategies, so the lessons learned are time tested and work. Whatever the reason, and I know from personal experience there are many, you need to take responsibility for negotiating the best possible terms. The goal is to do so consistently and successfully.

We've agreed: You're navigating your career through a strange and unfamiliar landscape. It's scary out there. You face increasing uncertainty in the markets, there are fewer opportunities to pursue, and among those that are available, there's an emphasis on expertise and specialization. Confidence has clearly shifted and so has your ability to gauge success. Is it still possible to play hardball when you negotiate? Yes, but you better know what you're getting yourself into before you ski the advanced slope. The economic collapse that began in 2008 with the credit crunch, bear markets, and unemployment has clearly changed the rules. As a corollary, you have to change how you approach this process.

So, here is the theme for this chapter: negotiation strategies for success in managing your career. It's not just about getting the most right now—although that's tempting, too—it's about creating and building upon a sustainable platform. Whether your decision to move on is voluntary or involuntary or whether you're working or unemployed, real, live, negotiating skills that stand up when you're in the heat of the moment will protect your interests and enhance your reputation.

I can't be there with you when you're in the midst of managing a negotiation, but I can offer you a few ideas to do it better. I'm generally an optimist, which translates into: Yes, I believe that there's always some room to negotiate. Right at this moment, if I were you, I'd be thinking about the following "how's and why's:"

- How is it possible to negotiate in a lousy market?
- How do I distinguish myself from others competing for the same position?

- What is my value proposition and why?
- Don't I face a disadvantage now that the balance of power feels like it's shifted?
- What can I possibly negotiate for?

Let's discuss....

What Is Negotiation?

Despite its importance, negotiation is often misunderstood and mishandled. It's not intended to be adversarial, but because it's often viewed as such, it's a process that many of us prefer to avoid in the hope that the matter at hand resolves itself. You can be sure you'll be disappointed with the outcomes of situations where you back off on the tougher, more challenging issues. You may get an offer but not one you'll necessarily like.

First of all, let's agree on a definition of negotiating. It goes something like this: Whenever you're asked for information that you may not want to provide or you request information that may not be forthcoming or readily available, you're faced with a negotiation decision. Negotiation is essentially an exchange. What do you have or want, how important is it to you, and what boundaries have you established regarding how much or how little you're willing to compromise? It's the same from their side of the table...whoever they may be. During negotiations, you should know your walk-away point, but work hard to avoid it, unless you have other desirable options in your back pocket. A good and successful outcome allows you and whoever you're working with to feel like you've both achieved fair, reasonable, and acceptable terms. It also feels like the experience has been collaborative. It should rarely involve ultimatums.

Negotiation sometimes feels like the end result of a successful job search. Clearly, it's not. It's on-going and persistent throughout every step of your interviews and your life at work. As I mentioned earlier, it begins in job search when someone asks you for something that you would prefer not to give. There are four basic steps to negotiation, and they generally unfold in the following sequence. This Four-Step Salary Negotiation Method was developed by The Five O'Clock Club, Inc., a national career counseling organization, and is printed with its written permission (www.fiveoclockclub.com):

1. **Negotiate the job or role first.** Your goal is to create an opportunity for yourself that maximizes your potential to be both successful and satisfied. That means a role in which you're viewed as the ideal candidate. It's a collaborative process, and it will require that early on you take the lead. As you present your unique qualifications and skills, it should become apparent to the hiring manager that the role you're interviewing for will need to be modified. Once that happens, it's just a matter of time.

2. **Outshine and outlast the competition.** Negotiating tactics are critical to help you execute a winning job search strategy. The job search process is a marathon, and negotiation is one more skill that keeps you in the race. Job search is a lot of work and at times it feels like there's more work than results. You need to know who you're competing against to figure out how to outsmart them. Who is the ideal candidate and what are the qualities and characteristics that make them special? How can you transform yourself into that candidate? Someone has to win as long as the job doesn't disappear. Why shouldn't it be you?

3. **Get the offer.** That's the goal, right? You want to get as many offers as possible and select the offer that positions you both for the immediate future, and ensures that you remain attractive and employable over the long term. Far too many clients react impulsively to an offer, and end up making a bad decision. So, while you're interviewing, you should also be gathering a lot of information on which to base your decision. *How will my success be measured? What kinds of skills and qualifications will be acquired? Will these be valuable for me as my career unfolds? Will I like what I'm doing? How solid is the company?*

It's your career, and every decision you make must be based on a careful and rigorous evaluation...and even then, there's no guarantee that it's going to work out. All you can do is make an informed decision and hope for the best. If it's a bust, I can assure you that it's infinitely easier to explain a rational decision that may have tanked than an impulsive one that just "felt" right.

4. **Negotiate the salary.** Yes, this is the very last stage. Of course, you will find yourself negotiating one thing or another from the beginning of your conversations. It's salary that I'm referring to here. Salary information may be requested early on, and that's OK. You should try to avoid disclosing any numbers. It's just an unnecessary distraction that provides no real meaning or value to the hiring manager or recruiter. Give it to them if they really need to know. It doesn't make much of a difference. What you tell them now will be modified when they realize how valuable you have the potential to be. It will also be modified when they compete against another company to win you. So never, ever negotiate your compensation until after the offer is officially presented. It's impossible for the company to know your real potential to contribute and to add value...and you certainly don't have as much power either.

But First, a Few Universal Rules

1. Negotiation involves risk...you never know the outcome until you reach that point in the discussion. No matter how creative your strategy and techniques are that you deploy, there is always the very real potential for the negotiation to break down. Job search is also about managing rejection. You need to establish realistic metrics to evaluate your progress and measure your success and recognize that it's dangerous to take the rejection personally.

2. If you can't afford to walk away from the conversation, you have very little room to negotiate. If you need a job right now—it's urgent—then don't be dumb and jeopardize the offer by negotiating aggressively. Remember, you can continue to job search after you've landed, or you can develop a strategy to improve your situation once you're on the job. Still, know your walk-away point even in a negotiation of limited potential.

3. On the other hand, there is generally a little room to wiggle. Most offers that are presented assume that you will negotiate, even if it's just to show them that you have a pulse. As a Wall Street professional, the negotiation is an important opportunity to demonstrate that you can confidently represent yourself and your interests...just as you will be expected to do on behalf of the company.

4. Negotiation begins at the very beginning of your job search, not at the tail end. When you're asked a question, any question, you have started to negotiate your relationship. For example: In a job posting, it might be a request for salary history and expectations, with a recruiter a list of references early on in the process, or in an interview for a position you want it could be the name of your current or most recent manager to contact. You may also find yourself scrambling to prepare for performance reviews. Yes, these are all examples of negotiation.

5. Job search and career management are not linear. When we have options, we have power. When you approach a single opportunity and invest all of your attention and energy on seeing that option through to its conclusion *and* you neglect other opportunities, you make yourself far too vulnerable. It is also extremely inefficient. Juggling multiple conversations may be a lot more challenging especially in a tough market, but at least it creates a competitive energy that surrounds you in your search. Besides when you focus on a single option, it's highly likely that

it will disappear. The odds are against you in a tough market, no matter how great you may be as a candidate.

6. These principles are only the beginning. Any real negotiation demands a careful and thoughtful examination of the opportunity, your unique situation, your level of comfort, and the parameters that are reasonable.

7. Most of us are not naturally gifted negotiators. Trust me...you get better and more confident with practice.

Lesson One: The Job Search Affection Curve

This is not a lecture on probability or statistics. In fact, if it were, current data would suggest that the potential to negotiate successfully is highly unlikely. I don't agree. The Job Search Affection Curve is all about managing relationships...and your goal in job search is to establish many of these.

What is the Job Search Affection Curve? It is quite simply a timeline...with time in job search measured along the x-axis. For the purposes of this explanation, and for this explanation only, we examine your conversations with a single company. The y-axis represents your progress in getting that company to see you as infinitely desirable.

Over time, you establish the relationship, you nurture and cultivate the relationship, and then you reach a point where the relationship either moves forward or it doesn't. It's a lot like dating. If you follow the rules, define boundaries early on, and convey your level of activity and the interest it generates to all the folks you're talking to, you will reach what I refer to as the "point of no return." They—the company—have decided that you're the one. It's the Sally Field "you really love me" moment. They've fallen in love with you. Virtually nothing you say or do now will jeopardize your status.

Now it's your turn. You have the power to ask for what you want. Is it foolproof? No. Is it irreversible; does the process have the potential to break down? Yes. It can stop dead in its tracks. That's why you need strategy and patience to see it through. You also need good humor to ensure that you haven't boxed yourself into a corner where any further request you make will be viewed as an ultimatum.

How do you know when you've reached this point? I can't tell you precisely, but what I can offer is a way to manage it once you find yourself there. I can also suggest what it may feel like to be in the driver's seat.

Tom and David

Let's compare two bankers, Tom and David, who were clients of mine in job search. Tom was passive. He pursued only one job at a time and, for better or worse, that's all he was comfortable doing. It's the "all of my eggs in one basket" approach. Great if it works out but devastating if someone inadvertently sits on the egg carton. What enormous pressure to make every interview a home run and to anticipate every possible land mine. This is never a recommended strategy if your goal is to facilitate negotiation.

David was much more resourceful. He pursued several opportunities at the same time and knew that most of them would fall away through absolutely no fault of his. David shared his status, success, and excitement with each of his key stakeholders. These were the people and companies he was talking to no matter how early on in the interviewing process. His intention was to get each of them to see him as a great and desirable candidate even if the job may have ultimately disappeared. It's not arrogance that motivated David. It was a sincere belief that he was uniquely qualified and suitable and deserved to be taken seriously.

Of course, whenever you communicate important information to your audience, it needs to be presented carefully and respectfully. It's far too easy to cross over from candidate to pest. Like David, you have to be convinced that this information is vital so that each of the companies is aware of where you and they stand. Only report on your progress when you've made progress...not before, and please do so on an ongoing basis. How else will each company know of your potential, and David's, to be snapped up? By feeding this information selectively, you're helping them to make the very best possible decision regarding you as a candidate.

Lesson Two: Managing Multiple Conversations

The way you create demand for yourself is by pursuing multiple opportunities at once. This approach produces the kind of dynamic energy that is critical to success in negotiating. Visually, it's like a wagon wheel.

You're at the center of this wheel, and each spoke represents a different opportunity. Ideally, you have at least four to six spokes at any single point in time. An opportunity can range from a "getting to know you" conversation with a firm to final-round interviews. Remember that you're continuing to feed information to each of these spokes about your status and any developments that have the potential to make you unavailable.

Tom's job search lacked energy and so did his interviews. What could he talk about beside himself and his interest in the company? Companies get this, and when they do, any sense of urgency about you as a candidate disappears in a heartbeat. Whether Tom was working or not, there was really no need for his interviewers to move quickly. What was the point? He'd still be there.

David, on the other hand, made sure that each of the four or five companies he was in talks with knew about any important developments: *Hi, it's been a while since we last spoke and I wanted to bring you up-to-date on how a few of my conversations have unfolded. I continue to be very interested in your firm and I thought it would be helpful for you to know what's going on.* When interviews were being scheduled, he would tactfully convey his level of activity and potential to be unavailable: *Gee, I'm delighted to be meeting with John and Lisa. Tomorrow and Thursday are kind of tough, I already have meetings scheduled. How about Wednesday afternoon?* It's a subtle way for David to show that he's busy, that he's attractive to other companies, and that he's not relying too heavily on any single conversation to be "the one."

Companies always sense your level of neediness, which can work to your advantage. When you shift the balance of power like this, you make it a lot easier for the company to like you and want you. The goal is to be seen as great and as infinitely desirable. When you make this happen—and it's not as difficult as you might think—then you don't have to formally negotiate. It's a consequence, a by-product, of a successful job search.

Negotiation Strategies

Let's focus now on negotiation strategies. As I mentioned, negotiation begins when you're asked for information that may have the potential to eliminate you from consideration. That can happen when you first make contact with a company, and they ask you to provide compensation numbers, history, or expectations. A job posting might specify that as a requirement to be considered as a candidate, or a recruiter may demand to know. How to respond is a subject of great debate.

However you open up your discussions with a prospective employer, no matter what they may ask, a negotiation means you can modify and change your positions as the interview process unfolds. So, it's not really a big deal from my perspective. It's not that you should mislead. Just know that the more you interview at a single company, the more time and interest they've invested in you. If possible, try to hold off from giving numbers for as long as possible. Here are a couple of examples:

- I was expecting that you'd want to have a conversation about numbers, and I'm delighted to share that information with you. I'm very familiar with the salary range for this position, and it's where I was assuming I'd fall. *And if you've been introduced to the company by a recruiter, you might add the following:* The recruiter has also shared this information in detail with me.

- It feels so early in the interviewing process. I was hoping that we'd have the opportunity to get to know each other a little better. It's not that I'm unwilling to share that information...in fact, it's critical. But I'm really hoping we'll get better acquainted first. That way you can really assess my background and qualifications without any distractions.

- Salary is not a priority for me at this point in my career. What's most important is to find a meaningful role and a stable home. I've done my research. I know what these positions pay. I've had conversations with folks here at the bank. I'm sure you'll all be fair. Of course, salary is important, but it's really secondary.

At the end of the day, if they really insist on knowing, give it up: *My compensation in this past year was* —————. If you suspect that the position is paying less than you were earning, just give your base. If you think it's a lot higher, make sure to lump together your base and bonus. Remember, it's not a debate. Your goal is to get another meeting and not to win in a conversation. It's never appreciated, and it will bite you in the ass. You may win the debate, but you'll lose the war. Besides, any numbers you give are only meaningful right now, at this moment in time.

Jennifer

For Jennifer, a soft market required a re-evaluation of the level of compensation she could expect. It wasn't that the overall compensation would necessarily be changing. It was the number upfront that a firm would be willing to commit to, both in terms of total compensation and base salary. Jennifer is an institutional salesperson, and she has deep experience and knowledge in a very specialized product. When she found herself out of work—the first time in her career—due to the bankruptcy of her firm, she was effective in tapping immediately into a large network of colleagues, clients, and friends in the industry. She had never worked anywhere else and the numbers that were being presented to her felt unreal. How could the compensation have changed so dramatically?

Jennifer was stuck in terms of how to best respond to the salary question. She was asked again and again: What are you looking for? She was afraid to disclose her real salary history for fear that it would make her look too expensive. On the other hand, she was concerned about coming across as not forthcoming. What could she possibly be hiding? For Jennifer, salary was just a number, but now that number felt like a big problem.

If Jennifer was asked at the beginning of her conversations what she was expecting, here's how she addressed the question:

> I'm very concerned about either under- or overpricing myself. I'm sure you can appreciate that. Here's what I can bring to this role and to your firm —————— [for Jennifer, here's where she would describe her qualifications, skills, and perspective on how to build the business. For you, it's a fill in the blanks]. What would that translate into in terms of compensation? What do you envision?

Or an alternative and more direct response:

> The market is strange. You must have a number in mind. What's the range?

When Jennifer received her first offer, it wasn't what she expected. The compensation was weighted heavily on incentives. She knew that it would take a while to build the business but the base would barely cover her monthly nut. It was a distraction that she preferred to avoid. Besides, dipping into her savings would mean working under an unrealistic and unclear deadline. Here's how Jennifer approached this point in the negotiation:

> I think that you'll agree...I bring a unique set of skills and qualifications to this role. It's a business that I've already established. I know that it has enormous potential to really grow. I have absolutely no doubt that the market remains strong enough to support this growth. That's why I'm hoping we can agree on a formula for compensation that would allow me to focus all of my attention on building this business. I have financial obligations, and I'd hate to be distracted.

The Offer

You've received the offer. Maybe it's surprisingly good, even great, far beyond your wildest imagination. To ask for more or to haggle over minor points would seem piggy. I agree. I would hope that all of you have the good fortune to face this prospect...but it's unlikely. No, allow me to be even more emphatic. There's not a snowball's chance in hell. The market sucks, and you work in an industry based on winning and losing. The numbers won't add up.

It would be unwise and reflect poorly on the firm for an employer to give you their best offer right out of the gate. You wonder why? A crappy firm negotiates badly. It's not just embarrassing—it suggests that they're unskilled as negotiators. It's a bad sign for things to come, both for you and for the firm. A generous company isn't necessarily a smart one. If you're thinking long term, you want to work for a company that produces an offer that's based on a logical and systematic evaluation. The offer makes sense given their needs, yours, and the reality of the market. A pushover may give you all that you want right now, but for how much longer? Alternatively, a firm that is inflexible is not capable of recognizing the real value you bring. If they're not willing to show some enthusiasm from the very start of the relationship, it doesn't bode well for how they'll treat you over time.

The truth is, I've never worked with a client who received an offer that couldn't be improved upon. Whether or not they wanted to, that's another issue. There is always some wiggle room. It's not just about compensation, bonus, severance, or relocation. It could be as little as a start date. I know the market is tough, and there's real fear and legitimate concern about how much latitude we actually have to negotiate. It's a tough call, and one that I can't make for you. I will emphasize that how you're perceived from the start has great bearing on how you'll be treated once you're in place. Negotiate with confidence and respect, and you have the potential to enhance your image and authority.

When the offer is presented, you and the company have an opportunity now to size each other up. In negotiating objectively, you need to do your homework. What do these positions pay? What's the range? Where does this firm tend to fall within that range? To achieve success, you need to have an understanding of the parameters. If you don't, there's the potential to either over- or underprice yourself and to be disqualified for the wrong reasons.

What do you say when you receive a gift? Thank you, of course. What happens when you receive a bad gift? It's the exact same response. Even a bad gift deserves to be acknowledged. That's what happens when you receive an offer. We thank the person extending the offer and express our sincere gratitude. It's also important to convey that you need a little time to digest the information and to tie up a few other loose ends. Notice how I've introduced very gently the idea that you have other conversations that need to be handled responsibly. It's not meant to introduce stress into the equation or to present an ultimatum. It's just valuable information that the company making the offer must have in order to take you seriously.

Sam

Sam grew up in mainland China and moved to the United States as a teenager. He spoke virtually no English when he arrived. He's a bright fellow and excelled in high school despite the language barriers.

Even today, he still has a very heavy Chinese accent. Sam received a full scholarship to college, where he studied engineering. He was a member of the campus ROTC program, Reserve Officers' Training Corps, and upon graduation, he joined the U.S. Navy. He spent the next six or seven years on a nuclear submarine and eventually rose to become the Assistant Commander. You don't interact with people much when you're below water and in the role of technical specialist, so Sam's language skills remained weak. That's precisely the reason why I offer his story as an illustration. It inspires. If he can negotiate successfully, so can you.

After the military, Sam attended a top business school, spent a summer in Washington, DC working for the Department of the Navy, and then joined a money center bank after school. It wasn't his ideal choice but few opportunities were presented to him through the on-campus recruiting process. Translation: He never made it to second-round interviews. Sam worked in a group that was involved in structuring transactions. He was the credit expert. Sam lost his job when the bank was "merged" in a hostile take-over. We met after he had been unemployed for 12 months.

It would not be an understatement to say that Sam was at his wits' end. Beyond all else, he shared with me his feelings of failure and a profound belief that he had brought dishonor and shame to his family. I asked Sam the standard questions in getting to know a new client: what kind of job he was looking for and how he had conducted his job search. He explained to me that he wanted to use his separation from the bank to finally pursue the kind of job he wanted back at business school. His goal was to work in M&A as an investment banker, to do so as a lateral move, to make more money, and to join a top-tier institution in NYC. It's no surprise that he was out of work for a year. In fact, he hadn't even been invited for a single interview. Sam's list of criteria was virtually unattainable. Because language barriers made networking a challenge, he also relied heavily on responding to job postings. Even in the best of times, finding a job in M&A is like looking for a needle in a haystack. Positions were rarely posted, and if they were, they were at a level that Sam felt was far below where he deserved to be.

I gave Sam a homework assignment that he and I would both do. We had to find at least five jobs that were advertised, and then together we would prepare a boilerplate letter for his response. A week later, we met. I had identified seven jobs and—no big surprise—he found none. Why not? Each of the jobs I presented was either too junior or not geographically desirable. That was the first of our many disagreements...or as I prefer to see them now, milestones for learning and behavior change. He was tough.

One of the job postings was for a position based in Cleveland. It was an Associate-level position in M&A for a newly established investment bank, a subsidiary of a regional bank. Sam was mortified. Cleveland, Associate, regional bank! He had seen the same ad and chose to ignore it. I, on the other hand, felt that he could benefit from as much interview practice as possible. Besides, you never know if an opportunity is right for you until the conversations begin. Despite considerable resistance, I insisted that Sam respond to the posting.

The posting, like many, requested salary history and expectations. But unlike other postings, this one included the cap for compensation. This was a little odd, but at least we had an idea how to position Sam. He was not happy because the top of the range was far below where he expected and wanted to be. So how did he respond? In the very last paragraph of his letter, here's what he wrote:

> I would be pleased to meet with you to discuss my background and qualifications in greater detail. At that time, I would also be happy to share comprehensive salary history and expectations.

Remember, whenever you negotiate, you make the decision as to whether you're willing to walk. In Sam's case, he felt that the position was beneath him, so it was a non-issue. If you can't afford to be as stubborn as Sam, then I encourage you to provide the information that's been requested...but do so in a way that doesn't jeopardize you as a candidate. Make sure you've done your homework and know the prevailing salary range for this type of position and also take into account regional differences in compensation and cost of living. Fortunately, the posting provided this information, so Sam had a benchmark to play with. With or without this information, consider the following:

- Providing a range:

  My goal is to secure a position that offers a base salary between —————— *and* ——————.

- Providing past salary history but in the context of the posting:

  In my most recent position, I was earning a base salary of —————. *I know and sincerely believe that this is an exciting opportunity, and I want to emphasize that salary is not a priority at this point in my career* [that's not to say that salary won't be a priority tomorrow, a week from today, or next month...but at this very moment in time, I want that damn job].

I suspected that if Sam met most of the criteria in the posting, there was a strong possibility that he would be contacted by the company. Sam's letter hit all of the requirements. He was trained at a well-respected New York institution. We also modified his resume to emphasize his ability to contribute immediately and, given the fact that this was a start-up initiative, his ability to wear many hats. If Sam were to be contacted, I also assumed that it would be handled by the HR person as the initial screener and most likely through a phone call or via e-mail. I wanted to make sure that Sam was prepared for this conversation.

Sam did, in fact, receive a phone call from the HR person. What did she ask for almost immediately? Yes, salary information:

Sam, we love your background but don't know if we can afford you. What is your salary history, and what are your expectations?

Under any other circumstances, Sam would have told her what he had earned and what he wanted. All or nothing...he would have ignored any potential to find a middle ground. Fortunately, I had already scared him sufficiently. *It's been a year. Nothing you've done so far has produced or will produce results. Do you want to work? Are you willing to do whatever it takes to make that happen?* These kinds of questions became our mantra, but were needed less frequently as Sam gained some momentum and confidence.

Here's how Sam responded to the HR person's question. Let me also emphasize that what you read here, however simple in its delivery, is the by-product of many hours of practice. Sam had a lot of bad habits that needed to be broken!

> I was expecting that at some point we'd have this conversation about salary history and expectations. I'm delighted to share any and all numbers with you. My hope, though, is that we can get to know each other a little bit better first. Let me reassure you, I've done my homework. I know what this sort of position pays, and I'm comfortable with it. I'm sure you'll be fair.

This became Sam's mantra, and you're welcome to borrow it, too:

> I've done my homework. I know what this position pays. I'm comfortable with it [for right now]. I know you'll be fair.

Sam did know what the position paid. The cap for compensation was provided in the ad. That was good fortune but not entirely necessary. With minimal research, he could easily have determined the range. Remember, it was too early for Sam to negotiate the numbers but not so early to come across as a reasonable, smart candidate. Did he mislead by suggesting that he could live with the compensation? From my perspective: No. The company has no idea yet how valuable Sam will be, and this protects them from making a bad decision based solely on the numbers. It also gives Sam some time to pursue other conversations. At the end of the day, he needed a job, even if the compensation was below what he considered acceptable. Better, too, that the decision be in his court than theirs.

If you're pinned down, remember that it's not a debate. Give it up. You can always change your salary expectations later on in the process once you begin to generate real momentum. If possible, before you share any numbers, try to get a range:

> This is an important move for me. I'd hate to either over- or underprice myself. Is it possible to get a range?

And if the range that's offered is OK for now:

> That's exactly where I was expecting you'd be. I'm entirely comfortable with the numbers.

If the range is below where you'd like to be, but you want the interviews to continue:

> I'm very excited by the prospect of working here and, in particular, my potential to add real value in this role. As you know, my compensation has been a little higher than what you're paying. I believe any decision we make involves opportunity costs. Compensation is not an issue for me right now.

Let's get back to Sam. Our strategy worked. He was invited to Cleveland for a full day of interviews. He met with the entire senior leadership team. His first conversation was with the newly appointed division president. What happened? The very first question he asked Sam had to do with salary: *I don't see anything here about your compensation. Coming from New York, you must be well-paid.* He was presenting Sam with a challenge, and Sam responded as he had with the HR person in their phone conversation a few days before. He repeated his mantra: *homework, knowledge, comfortable, and fair.* By now, you know the drill. This time around, he also added: *As you may know, I've already addressed compensation with the HR person.* In truth, he responded to her question, but he didn't provide her with numbers.

By the end of the day, Sam had been asked by three of his interviewers about compensation. Not once did he disclose either what he had earned or what he was looking for. He left Cleveland that evening, and by the very next morning, he had already e-mailed his follow-up correspondence. Late that afternoon, he received a call from the HR person. It was a home run. They loved him. Not only did he match all of the skills that they felt were critical to success in the position, but he also brought additional experience that would be invaluable for this start-up, an important point to note as he moved forward in the negotiation.

Fortunately, I prepared Sam for the possibility of an offer. Remember our discussion about bad gifts? Well, Sam felt that he had been screwed. I reminded him that it was impossible for the bank to present an offer to him that reflected his expectations. At no time did he share what he was expecting. So, when Sam received the offer, he thanked the HR person profusely. He also expressed his gratitude, and he made it clear that he would need additional time to finalize conversations elsewhere.

With respect to actually negotiating the offer, I insisted that he meet in person with the organization and with the individual officially designated to have this conversation. Cleveland was an easy trip, and if Sam wanted to make a stronger impression and to drive home his commitment to joining them, he needed to be there. It's always more effective to have this sort of conversation in person if logistically possible. Telephone or e-mail allows the person you're negotiating with to assume a tougher, take-it-or-leave-it approach. It's a lot easier to disengage by phone: *OK, it sounds like we've reached an impasse. Why don't we agree to disagree? Have a good life.* By sitting with them and physically being there, it forces accountability and responsibility.

So here's what Sam said to the HR person:

Thank you so much. I'm deeply honored and grateful for the offer and I'm looking forward to working with you [yes, he can say this without misleading or suggesting that he's accepted the offer...he is looking forward to working with them, but only if they agree on terms and conditions]. *As I may have mentioned to you, I have a few loose ends that need to be tied up, and I just need a couple of days to make that happen. In the meantime, may I have the offer in writing? I'd also like to sit down with you or my new boss because I'm sure I'll have several questions. When are you free? How about next Tuesday or Wednesday? Again, I want you to know how excited I am to have received this offer.*

The next week Sam returned to Cleveland to meet with both the HR person and his new boss. To prepare for the conversations, I asked him to list all of the items that he wanted to negotiate, their order of importance to him, and why. Here's his list of priority, beginning with the most important first:

1. Salary
2. Title
3. Relocation
4. Sign-on bonus

For each of these items, Sam needed to justify why he deserved them and what he brought to the table. Earning a certain amount of money in the past doesn't entitle you to earn the same in the future. You need to demonstrate why you're worth what you're asking for. For salary, it was clear that Sam would be offering much more in the way of skills and experience than the original job posting had required. He could hit the ground running, and he also had the potential to wear many hats, a valuable asset in a newly established business.

With respect to title, Sam had been a vice president at his former institution, and he was now being offered one as an associate. With these expanded responsibilities and client contact, it was indisputable that a VP title would carry greater credibility. On a personal level, Sam could not and would not consider making a move to be an associate. He viewed that as a move backward professionally, and it was just unacceptable. Was it right or wrong to let his pride be a roadblock to a job? Not for me to judge. Instead, he and I needed to build a defensible strategy to support his requests.

Number 3, relocation, is standard operating procedure at most companies when a candidate lives more than 50 miles from the office.

Sam would be moving from Manhattan, and he needed to have the expense covered—for the actual physical move and for related costs of set up, including real estate fees for a rental, temporary housing, and so on. Policies vary from company to company, and Sam wanted to make sure that he was not out of pocket for the move.

Last, but not least, Sam was hoping to receive a sign-on bonus. For the uninitiated, that's a gift given to a candidate for deciding to join a company. It's intended to sweeten an offer. It could be used as an incentive or encouragement to choose one company over another or just as a way to demonstrate that the company really wants you there. It was a long shot, but why not? He now had a seat with them at the table, and it was his least-important item to negotiate. Why did he deserve a sign-on? That's a valid question. Sam did not have another offer to use as leverage, and it was also a tough time in the economy. Quite simply, the bank placed the ad directly and incurred no recruiter expense. They were also hiring a uniquely qualified candidate with a skill set far beyond what they had initially thought they needed. Sam was like a gift with purchase. He brought additional skills and experience that could be exploited to the bank's advantage.

As far as order goes, I felt that it was much more effective for Sam to begin with the big items first—get them out of the way and use the secondary requests as a back-up if he needed to compromise. I also felt that if Sam began his discussion with the less-important matters, by the time the negotiation conversation turned to what was most important to him, the bank would feel that he was asking for far too much. *We've already agreed to pay for your relocation. What more do you want from us?* By starting with the big stuff, the other items would feel insignificant and so much more likely to be approved.

The benefit of hindsight is that I can summarize the events that unfolded. Sam's conversation with the HR person went something like this:

> Thanks again for spending time with me. I wanted to express to you how genuinely excited I am about the opportunity to join the bank and how much I really appreciate the offer. This is incredibly exciting. I've given a great deal of thought to the offer, and there are a couple of items that I'd like to discuss with you.

Notice, he used the word "items" and not "issues" or "challenges." Items are open to discussion, whereas issues and challenges need to be resolved. Please also note that Sam made sure to thank them yet again for the offer...it's always good to begin a negotiation with some demonstration of your gratitude and showing how great a person you are. It's much easier to say no to a jerk.

> First and foremost, I'd like to talk to you about the salary. As I think became clear in our meetings, I bring a lot more to the table than you originally planned. It's my belief that the salary may not reflect this expanded responsibility. I'm hoping that's something you'll re-visit.

This is a reminder to both the HR person and to Sam's boss that the meetings produced important insights into Sam's ability to make significant contributions to the business. He's stating a fact here. This is indisputable. It's also a reasonable request.

> A second item that I'd like to discuss is the title. As you know, I'll also have immediate and expanded client contact. That's great! I'm confident, based upon my past experience, that I'll be able to make an immediate contribution. From this experience, I've found that having a position as an officer makes a huge difference with respect to being taken seriously by clients...more so than being an associate.

If salary and expanded responsibilities are presented first, and there's agreement all around as to their importance, it's only logical that a more senior title be considered. Again, the way to justify more money and a bigger title is by presenting a defensible strategy. Sam's logic could not be debated.

As you know, I currently live in NYC. There's an expense involved in relocating to Cleveland. What is the bank's policy?

Because we knew that a bank of this size would have a reasonable relocation policy, it seemed unnecessary to present this as a starting point. There was no need to have them agree to a condition that would have been provided anyway.

Finally, I'm wondering if the bank would be receptive to a sign-on bonus. It's common practice for institutions like this one to offer a candidate an incentive to join. It would make it an easy decision for me.

Why not ask for as much as you can get? As long as you've done your homework and know that your request is reasonable and customary for your industry and role, then there's no harm...as long as it's not presented as an ultimatum. In this case, Sam reminded them that he was found through a posting on a job board. No recruiter fee was incurred, which could have involved many thousands of dollars.

The result: Sam discovered that biases can often cloud good judgment. He approached this opportunity with great skepticism and virtually no interest. The outcome surprised him and even more unexpected was the decision he ultimately made. The HR person came back to him a day later with a revised offer and acknowledgement that the overall package needed to be re-configured. It was in large part due to Sam's very convincing and logical approach to the negotiation discussion.

Here's what the bank responded with: an increase in the base of $15,000, a title of vice president, and a lump sum payment of $25,000 to serve as a combined relocation reimbursement and sign-on bonus. It could be used in any way Sam wanted. He was thrilled! Was it a perfect offer and situation? No. But it did get Sam closer to where he wanted to be over the long term: a career in M&A. It was about as good as it could get.

Sam, Part Two

About six months after Sam joined the bank, all hell broke loose. Virtually everyone was fired except for the division president and Sam. It wasn't that Sam was more important than his colleagues. He was just lucky. His boss knew that and so did Sam. He was the point-person on a big transaction that had the potential to produce substantial revenue for the bank...as long as a few critical elements remained in place. Sam called me immediately. He knew that once the transaction was completed, he would no longer be valuable to the bank or to his boss. He also felt that this represented a unique once-in-a-lifetime opportunity to re-negotiate his situation.

What was Sam looking for? More money, a higher-level title, a percentage of the transaction when it closed (that is, a success fee), an incentive to continue working at the bank instead of beginning an active job search, and severance plus outplacement when and if his role wound down. These were all fair requests but a lot to swallow in the aftermath of the organizational meltdown.

Sam was concerned how to best present what he wanted. So, here's how we proceeded. Like the first round of negotiation, Sam prioritized what he was hoping to get. But this time, I changed the rules. I asked him to begin with the least-important items first. Why? I felt that the situation at the bank was tense enough and that the division president, now Sam's boss, needed to be fed these items in small and very gentle doses. On the other hand, we also knew that Sam had his new boss over a barrel. By starting with the easy stuff first, Sam could then build a logical and convincing strategy. You'll see how he approached the discussion. First, the list of items, as follows:

1. Title

2. Compensation

3. Percentage of the transaction (a success fee)

4. Bonus

5. Severance

6. Outplacement

Sam had very little prior day-to-day contact with the president, who was reputed to have a short fuse. Sam was nervous but not enough to back off. Remember, use compliments and gratitude first as a technique to position the tougher stuff to follow. Not smarmy or insincere...genuinely grateful.

> I want to speak to you about the situation here. First of all, thank you for making a place here for me. It means a lot. You've got your hands full, and I want you to know that you have my undivided support.
>
> As I said, I want to talk to you about the situation. In light of all of the cuts, the fact that I'll be wearing even more hats, and my potential to generate substantial revenue through this transaction and another I'm working on, I'd like my title to be raised to Managing Director. That way, I'll have even more credibility with clients...both current and hopefully those in the future.

Yes. That was his boss's response. Easy enough, because there were only two of them now. It was simple to give Sam a promotion, just a bookkeeping entry. At that point, Sam and I knew that he had hooked his boss.

> That's great! Terrific! Since I'll be working a lot harder, and with a higher-level title, I'm sure the bank has a salary range for this new grade. What will my base be increased to?

Sam was getting a lot bolder in his requests. In truth, he had little to lose. Everyone else had been separated. It was only a matter of time for him. Besides, he knew at a minimum that his colleagues received severance. He would, too. He also knew that his boss was desperate to close the transaction and collect a substantial fee. Sam wanted, and was determined, to collect a portion of that fee. It was only fair.

There's another item I'd like to discuss with you. The transaction I'm working on is likely to close at some point soon, and you may also know that I'm working on a second. It's customary in the industry, especially in smaller firms, to get a percentage of the deal. What can we do about that? It hasn't been clearly outlined yet.

Sam's boss was not pleased with the direction of the conversation.

How much do you want...5%...10%? And while we're at this, what else do you want from me?

Sam was coached to stay calm. This was a divorce he was negotiating. In a month or two, it would all be behind him, and he'd be a line item on a financial statement.

I was thinking in the range of 25%.

Thanks for bringing up the need to talk about a few other things. Yes, I believe I deserve a guaranteed bonus for my hard work and also because it's not clear when my end date will be. It's already March, and I could be here through year end, finalizing the details on this transaction and the smaller one. Also, I'd like to know that there's a fair severance package in place and an outplacement program to provide job search support, too.

Sam ended up with a promotion to Managing Director, a 15% success fee, a minimum guaranteed bonus of 50% of his base salary, six months severance, a six-month outplacement program, and payment for relocation back to NYC. Sam threw in the final item at the very tail-end. He was on a roll.

Negotiation for Cowards

You may be convinced that there is absolutely no room to negotiate or you're filled with fear that a wrong step could disrupt the entire process. If so, it's not my place to convince you to take a more aggressive approach to negotiation. It is my responsibility, however, to make sure that you examine every possible option and leave no stone unturned if you do choose to negotiate. That's why I offer a second strategy: the coward's approach. It's not meant to imply inferior, bad, or second rate—just passive. The intention here is for you to avoid at all costs appearing to take a hard line. It's to gently and diplomatically introduce an alternative in the most nonthreatening way possible.

Let me illustrate. I met Nancy well into her job search. She had been out of work for a while, at least six months. By the time she found her way to my office, two options in back-office operations had moved pretty far along. One was for a long-term consulting assignment at a major broker dealer, and the other was for a permanent position at a money center bank. Nancy made the mistake of not sharing her status with each of them. How were they to know that the other existed and that Nancy had the potential to get an offer that would make her unavailable? In the absence of that critical information, the conversations continued to amble along with no end in sight or sense of urgency.

Nancy was growing increasingly impatient with the process. I suggested that she speak to her second-choice option, the consulting assignment, and provide a status report. She did, and they came back immediately with an offer and an apology for the delay. Nancy was about to accept when I asked her if she had advised the bank about the offer. I already knew the answer, "no," so of course, I urged her to get on the phone. She called her contact there. He explained that he was splitting his time between London and New York, and as a result, many matters that were important had been placed on the back burner. He asked her to hold off for a day and promised to get back to her. He called less than an hour later with an offer. Nancy was about to accept when yet again I intercepted. Had she negotiated the numbers?

Nancy wanted to be working again and also to be in a permanent situation. I explained that negotiation did not necessarily involve an ultimatum as she feared. It could be as simple as asking if there was a little wiggle room. Nancy agreed to make the request but also threatened my life if the process were to break down. It was said in jest, I hope. Nevertheless, I, too, had a lot riding on this. Here's how she approached her soon-to-be boss:

> Colin, I'm absolutely thrilled to have the opportunity to work with you. And I'm looking forward to joining your team. I've been giving a lot of thought to how I'll be able to add value immediately. It would make it such an easy decision for me if there were just a little wiggle room with respect to compensation.

For those who are paralyzed by fear, please add the following:

> Regardless as to what you decide, please know that it's my intention to join the bank. The extra money would just make a big difference in terms of financial obligations and such.

What transpired? Nancy made the phone call literally word for word as above and Colin responded with:

> How much...$5,000...$10,000?

Within 30 seconds, Nancy negotiated a $10,000 raise for herself! Although career counselors are notorious for embellishing the details, it was as simple as that. Although I always recommend that negotiation be handled in person, in this particular case, it really didn't matter. Nancy had already accepted the position when she prefaced her request.

Negotiation Checklist

Here's a list of items that have the potential to be negotiated. It's not comprehensive. It's just intended to give you an idea of the range of items to consider. Of course, you need to take into account a number of matters when deciding on what you deserve and want: the current economy, the number of other options you have in the pipeline, your level of comfort and skill in handling the negotiation, and the role you expect to play. For most of you, and I include myself in this category, many of these items will be irrelevant:

- **Salary.**   Base compensation, bonus...know what the market will bear! Know where you stand in terms of skills, experience, and potential to add value quickly.

- **Sign-on bonus.**   When an offer is extended, this is a bonus that's provided upfront rather than back-ended. It's meant to be an incentive. It's also often used to make a candidate whole, such as covering a bonus that may get lost in transition, or stock options that may not have vested.

- **Severance.**   This is a surprisingly easy item to negotiate. It costs the company nothing—zero—if it's not exercised.

- **Outplacement.**   Same as above. Outplacement, for the uninitiated, is job search and career support that's provided when you get fired. Do your research on the various firms and ask for one that has a good reputation, not one that treats its clients like a factory assembly line.

- **Flex schedule.**   If the commute is oppressive or you have childcare issues, why not see if this is an option. It's best to research the company's history in providing flex schedules or working from home.

- **Start date.**   Do consider some time off between jobs or between job search and the start of a new job. You need the time to clear your mind, relax, and prepare for the new job. On the other hand, a start date that's too far out suggests a lack of interest. What's acceptable? Ask them.

- **Vacation.**   Yes, it is possible to negotiate for more vacation time. One of my clients explained that she gave 150% to her job and that's why she expected additional vacation time...to recharge the batteries. Another client, a fellow in equity derivatives, explained that he used part of his vacation time to attend educational programs and to teach...that it was important for him and for the business to be involved with thought leaders.

- **Relocation.**   Most companies have standard relocation packages. Just be prepared to know what your expenses will be so they're all covered.

- **Non-competes.**   These restrict you from working. Be very careful in agreeing to terms that could make it difficult or even impossible to support yourself and your family. Although the courts generally ignore non-competes, if you have to sue your old company, their pockets are far deeper than yours.

- **Garden leave.** If you separate from the company, either by your choice or theirs, you may be prevented from working for an extended notification period. Generally, this timeframe has been agreed upon in advance by you and your employer. Your severance should at least cover your time out.

- **Support/budget/resources.** If you'll be managing a budget, how will it be determined? What sorts of tools will be available to you to support your success? A Bloomberg terminal? Staff?

- **Reporting relationships.** Clarify who you'll be reporting to and who reports to you. The path to hell is often paved with good intentions and a lack of information.

- **Office.** Do you know which office will be yours, or if you're on the trading floor, what desk? One of my clients, an institutional salesperson, discovered on her first day that she was sitting next to a fellow aptly nicknamed Piggy. She was miserable from the start.

- **Office decoration.** It may not be politically correct, especially in this current environment...just speak to a few former Merrill Lynch execs...but it is sometimes available and expected for very senior people.

- **Timing of salary and performance reviews.** This is an item that has the potential to be negotiated if you feel like you're coming in below where you want to be or think you should be. A compressed review period provides a framework to equalize your salary to market. Just be careful with this one. A shorter timeframe means less time to achieve your objectives.

- **Stock options/equity.** It's a good idea to get the advice of a tax attorney and expert in evaluating options and potential equity ownership. Ask around among friends and peers for recommendations of a good person to advise you, someone who's been vetted in handling these sorts of transactions.

- **Wardrobe allowance.** Sounds silly, but if you make media appearances and represent your new firm before the public, you need to make a great impression.

- **Memberships.**   Having access to your peers both professionally and socially may be critical for success and standard operating procedure if you're higher up in the corporate food chain or your role is to schmooze clients. Know what sorts of options are most appropriate before you have this discussion. Industry groups, yes. Sponsorship in clubs, on the other hand, is generally available to a select few.

- **Conferences.**   Besides the educational benefits, attending conferences and events offers a good opportunity to build and maintain your network. It also keeps you up to date on emerging trends and industry gossip.

- **Publications.**   Some subscriptions cost several thousand dollars a year. If they're critical to your success, then make sure you negotiate to have access to them.

- **Auto allowance.**   Reimbursement for lease, parking, and gas. You pay particular attention to this category only if your job requires use of a car or you're at a level where it's a perk that's generally made available.

- **Expense account.**   Like other categories, T&E may be essential to your job or a perk tied to your seniority. Make sure that you are aware of industry and company standards before you introduce this as an item for discussion.

- **Educational/tuition assistance.**   This could be sponsorship for an executive MBA, continuing professional education, specialized training such as media training, day-to-day skills development, and so on.

- **Professional assistance: tax/financial planning/legal.**   As the formula for your compensation becomes more complicated, you may have a need for tax, legal, and financial advice. If you are leaving your company to join another, you may have to deal with penalties, lost bonuses, and equalization to make you whole. If you are relocating either domestically or overseas, your tax situation will be a mess. You will need outside advice, which is very expensive.

- **Insurance protection for liability/key man.** If you work for a small firm where the principal is critical to its success, you need to be protected in the event of an accident or death. If your role has the potential to expose you to significant liability—for example, a board position—then you need insurance, too.

10

References, Skeletons, and You

"If you can't get rid of the skeleton in your closet, you'd best teach it to dance," George Bernard Shaw wrote. That serves as an apt theme for our chapter on references, you, and your job search. Wherever you go, your reputation will follow you, and your former colleagues and bosses hold immense power to shape that reputation in how they speak about you through the reference process. In a job market where there's increased movement and competition—people and financial institutions are coming and going in record numbers—it's likely that you'll find yourself in transition at some point. Even if you're a top performer with years of great reviews, it's challenging to keep track of references when former colleagues, bosses, and friends fall below or off the radar screen. Social media sites help, but they're just a starting point. Ultimately, the burden rests on your shoulders to maintain these relationships.

If only that was the extent of it. The fact is that virtually every of one of us has a skeleton or two hidden in the closet. For the very few among us who have a clean track record *and* know their references well, it's still hard not to feel anxious when other people are talking about you. For the rest of us, we need to make those skeletons dance. That's why your references need to be managed and nurtured before, during, and after your job search. This process is stressful enough. Why add to it by neglecting the obvious: prepping your references, performing occasional damage control by well-intentioned references, and preventing unwanted feedback.

It would be great if you could always maintain good professional relationships. That's just not possible or realistic, especially when you've been involuntarily separated from your job—OK, fired. Maybe your boss was a "psycho" or you were a casualty of corporate politics. Maybe you screwed up. Whatever the reason, when you get fired, it's hard to be objective. You're human, and so are they.

Their decision may be unforgivable, but there's no room for hard feelings or revenge when your goal is to land quickly. That's the point, isn't it? This is a sensitive issue for me, too. I don't respond well to rejection. So, the following advice is dispensed with my sympathy, an understanding for the predicament you may find yourself in, and the knowledge that it's not easy to ignore feelings that may be legitimate. This situation isn't about your pride or your ego—it's about survival. Pride is BS when the stakes are this high. So, swallow your pride, and get ready to manage your former employer for the reference you need. You don't want a bad reference to end up disqualifying you. Imagine, after making it through to final-round interviews, having your potential employer reject you based on a message that could have been smoothed over or modified. I'd be devastated; so will you. Let's not allow this to happen.

This chapter is devoted to those of you who haven't always exercised good, sound judgment at work. For the rest of you—I'm guessing it's just a very small minority of readers who have an impeccable reputation—skip it. If you've tripped occasionally, as I have, then you've probably damaged a professional relationship or two. It's not too late to repair them. Read on.

The Rules (and They Matter)

The reference process is guided by formal and informal rules. As you approach the offer stage, you may be asked to submit the names of professional and sometimes personal references. Recruiters may even request this information when they begin their conversations with you. Because you don't know their motives yet, be cautious. It's an odd request to make early on, and quite frankly, unnecessary. There's also the potential for them to misuse the names you provide. We'll tackle how to handle headhunters and their need for references later in this chapter. For now, let's consider the basics.

It used to be that you only needed to provide an employer with references after you received a job offer. Typically, a list of names would be submitted almost as an afterthought. That model is no longer working. In this current market, companies and hiring managers have no room to make bad decisions.

The opportunity costs and actual expense of bringing in the wrong candidate are significant. Job requirements have become even more specialized, the bottom-line and budgets continue to shrink, and increasing numbers of candidates are willing to misrepresent themselves and their qualifications. That's why the time from initial interview to offer is now unbearably long. No one wants to be responsible for pulling the trigger when it comes to actually extending the offer. What if you, the candidate, screw up? What if you're a bad decision? It's an embarrassment that most managers would prefer not to be identified with. That's also why references are often checked for even the most routine hiring decisions.

What's the first step to managing this process successfully? It's to understand what references really are and how they function. Generally speaking, a *reference* is the feedback used by hiring companies and headhunters to reconfirm their belief in you. It can be as basic as dates of employment and graduation. It can also be a lot more complex and comprehensive: a rigorous assessment of your strengths, weaknesses, personality, and potential. It's generally a by-product of the level of the position and the size of the organization. As you move up in the food chain, the company that may hire you wants and needs to know more about you and your past. No secrets or surprises will be tolerated!

Here's how the formal process of reference checking typically unfolds. As you get closer to the offer stage, you'll be asked to submit the names of a couple of professional references. How many names, and who do you offer up? At a minimum, two or three names will suffice, but remember, bigger jobs and larger companies will require more. Think carefully about your choices. Former bosses and colleagues are generally expected. These are the people with whom you've worked closely. They know you and should be familiar with your on-the-job performance. Ideally, whoever you choose as a reference should like you and think that you walk on water. On the other hand, an indiscriminate reference who thinks that everything you've ever done is perfect offers no real value or insight. No matter how positive the feedback, it needs to show that the person giving it knows you well and understands both your strengths and weaknesses as a candidate. Of course, it's heavily weighted in your favor.

What will they say about you? You should have an idea. Are they crystal clear on what you want and why? Are they in agreement that you're well-qualified to pursue this goal? Managing references, much like your job search, needs to be approached strategically. It's an ongoing process that starts even before you've figured out what sort of job you want. It's a critical part of your search strategy, and it continues until you've landed in your new position.

Step 1

Generate a list of everyone you know who should—not could—serve as a reference. You need to establish a baseline below which a reference is not acceptable. Include current and former bosses, other senior level managers, peers, industry colleagues, vendors if relevant, and friends should a personal reference be requested. Dig deep! It's more about quantity first, not quality. You'll edit the list as you go along. Some of them will make terrific references whereas others will be mediocre at best. It's possible that a reference you thought you'd never consider might be perfect for a particular job target. A longer list will make it easier and faster for you to customize your options.

Step 2

Don't wait until you're asked to assemble your list. When references are requested, it's usually at a critical point in your conversations with a company. It always surprises me how senior people often neglect the obvious. It's usually for one of two reasons: not wanting to deal with the fallout and memory of a messy separation, or they're just lazy and unwilling to take the time to anticipate potential landmines. That's the "land on my feet" scenario. Winging it has worked for you in the past. Why shouldn't it continue to? It may. On the other hand, it may not. In highly competitive markets, are you willing to take the risk?

Whatever the reason, if you scramble at the last minute to get together what you know will inevitably be requested, you or one of your references could possibly shoot a nasty hole in your foot. Sloppiness will not be tolerated. Part of reference gathering is evaluating the appropriateness of your references; knowing how they feel about you and what they're likely to say. It also involves preparing them to be "reference ready" so that when they're called to speak about you they'll be on. You have far too much riding on how they'll represent you to rely on chance. This process needs to be managed closely.

Step 3

After you've assembled your list, now you need to get everyone's permission. You also need to vet what they'll say about you. Who you select for your list should vary according to each opportunity. These are your job search advocates, and they need to be customized around the type of job you're a candidate for. Look at it from an ROI perspective. The goal is to maximize the value of your references and their ability to support you so that you land successfully.

Call the people you're most comfortable using, explain your job search goals, and ask for their permission to serve as a reference. Make sure to get the following information:

- Current employer
- Job title
- E-mail address
- Phone number
- Best time to call

When you've reached final-round interviews—references are normally requested around this time—call each of your references again to describe the position and your qualifications. Now is also the time to remind them of some of the home-runs that you hit while working together. Make sure they're relevant. How your references perform will be viewed as a reflection on you. Your references are expected to be smart, too. That means knowing enough about you to speak with authority and insight.

Step 4

Defuse a bad reference. Anticipate problems that could arise if the wrong person is called. Agreed, it's better to maintain good professional relationships but that's not always possible. If some are damaged, you may be able to repair them. As difficult as it will be, you have no choice but to face the forces of evil. It's impossible to avoid your former adversaries when you're in job search. Future employers demand references. The challenge: How do you turn them into advocates? No matter how uncomfortable you may be in reaching out, it is irresponsible not to anticipate potential problems that could destroy an offer. When you fear the outcome, you eliminate the possibility of finding a resolution or at least neutralizing the situation.

How do you clear the air? It's simple. Call or e-mail these people and ask them if they'd serve as references. Yikes, that's a lot of bending over backwards. In re-establishing contact, you may be pleasantly surprised. Time has a tendency to moderate even the most intensely bitter feelings. It's likely that since you and this person parted ways, he or she may have been chastened by the events in the economy. Just about everyone has been, or knows someone, in transition. If you're not working, your old boss or colleague may have forgotten the circumstances surrounding your separation. Remember, their lives are busy, too. Or alternatively, they may feel guilty about what happened to you.

I'm not about to minimize the courage it takes to reach out like this. It's a big step to take. It's also a necessary one. You may fear the worst when, in fact, there's absolutely no fall-out. If you decide to contact these people, it's probably a good idea to script what you'd like to say in advance. Emphasize how important this request is to you both professionally and personally. You don't want to forget the key points. Having an outline or script to follow keeps you on track. Once you've made the call, and hopefully had the conversation, then follow-up with an e-mail outlining the highlights. It's intended to serve two purposes: as a reminder and as an implicit agreement to the information that's been shared.

Step 5

At this point, if the issues in your relationship are still not resolved, then the strategy and focus shifts away from you and your lousy boss to the company where you're a final-round candidate. Your goal now is to perform triage. It's to minimize the negative information your future employer might receive. Here are a couple of techniques for managing the "spin" if your former boss isn't willing to play nice. The theme is damage control:

- **Make your boss disappear.** It may be that your former employer, like many others these days, has a standard policy in place that prevents all employees from providing references. Explain that your boss, who's a great guy, and with whom you had a terrific relationship, follows this policy without exception. As an alternative, offer the name of another manager who's agreed to speak off the record on your behalf. This person should be at an equivalent level and role as your former boss.

- **The Midwest strategy: earnest, honest, and heart-felt.** This is the "aw shucks" approach, said with sincerity and looking directly in their eyes. When the new company asks for references, tell them that you've always had outstanding relationships with all of your former bosses except for one. Provide any important background information about your relationship briefly and professionally. Absolutely no anger, bitterness, or theatrical gestures. For example, a boss who was hired and immediately and systematically recruited her own team. Everyone understands that. Or a boss who was forced to take you on as a result of a reorganization. When further cuts happened, clearly there was no rabbi to protect you.

- **Re-direct the reference.** Here's where you offer background information that shows clearly and persuasively why a particular reference—your bad boss—is not the right person to contact. Say you reported to a manager for a short period of time (less than six months is a general guideline), that person is clearly not familiar with the quality of your work and with you as a person. Wouldn't it be more productive to speak to a manager who worked with you over an extended period of time? Of course!

- **Don't do anything.** It's possible that your former boss won't return a reference checking call.

Jeffrey: Bad Boss

Jeffrey was hired by a European investment manager to head up and to expand its operations in North America. He was recruited out of a large U.S. insurance company where he was a senior portfolio manager, and one of only three senior executives in line to be the company's chief portfolio manager and strategist. He was passed over for the promotion, and that left him feeling like he'd been shortchanged.

Around that time, he was contacted by a recruiter about an interesting opportunity: a recent start-up with a rich funding source, a guaranteed minimum compensation package that was far beyond what Jeffrey had ever earned, freedom and independence, and great people. At least, that's how it was represented by the recruiter. It was a step up in terms of responsibility. It also offered significant upside potential for successful performance. In his role at the insurance company, incentive-based compensation was virtually nonexistent.

One glitch: Jeffrey would be reporting to a general manager based at headquarters in London. That individual had also been recently recruited from outside the company and had not yet officially joined. He was winding down a non-compete and was scheduled to start a month after Jeffrey. The turnover seemed odd. *Why would two senior positions be open at the same time? Would it be possible to meet his new boss prior to making a decision? Why wasn't this fellow actively involved in the recruiting process?* All legitimate questions. Jeffrey's concerns were promptly and cheerfully addressed by the CEO:

- His position was essentially newly created to reflect a more significant commitment to growing the business in the States. The person who had been in that role was not viewed as being senior or strong enough to assume the expanded responsibilities. Although he was offered the number-two spot, he declined and chose to leave.

- His new boss was on an extended holiday and was physically unavailable to meet. They spoke briefly by phone but the call was cut short due to poor cell coverage. Jeffrey was reassured that he was on board with the hiring decision and that he was impressed with Jeffrey's qualifications and reputation.

Lesson: Don't accept at face value that what you've been told is entirely true. When you're making a major life decision like accepting a new job, get enough information to minimize the unknowns. You have far too much to risk, as Jeffrey discovered, by performing sloppy due diligence. Your career is really about your survival and decisions of this kind are significant. If you are told you need surgery, you'll get a second opinion. Yes, you may still need the procedure. On the other hand, you may also avoid a costly and unpleasant mistake. Measure twice, cut once.

Jeffrey would discover that working for an individual he barely knew proved to be problematic, especially from a long distance. His boss had no investment in his success and had most likely seen Jeffrey as an interim substitute until he was up and running in London. Jeffrey also discovered once he became better acquainted with his colleagues in NY that his predecessor's departure was not so smoothly executed. It was not the company's first expansion strategy in the United States—it was just called something different before. His relationship with his boss seemed to sour quickly. By month 12, the duration of his contract, he was the next casualty.

Although Jeffrey was not fired for cause—it was positioned as a re-organization—he was concerned about how his time there and separation would be handled. Internally, he knew that his former boss had repeatedly expressed dissatisfaction with his performance...not communicated to Jeffrey directly but off the cuff to many of his colleagues. He also knew that his boss was basing this smear campaign on unrealistic expectations that were never mutually agreed upon. Because it was not beneath his boss to say bad things, Jeffrey had reason to worry. He had begun to interview, and it was clear that his former boss and company would be contacted for a reference. How best to handle this?

"Best" is not a sure thing in a situation like this. At Jeffrey's level, there was no question that his former boss would be contacted. We also knew that as loose cannons go, his potential to inflict damage was great. As a first step, Jeffrey needed to suck it up and reach out to him. It was intended as a "no hard feelings" conversation. And yes, it was awkward and hard to make the call:

I wanted to catch up with you and let you know what I've been up to. First and foremost, I'm hoping all is well with you.

As you may have heard, I'm actively out in the market now, and I'm getting a pretty good response. People have begun to ask for references, and I wanted to see where you stand on that. How my separation is presented is critical to my success at this juncture.

Even if Jeffrey doesn't trust his old boss, he still needs to get a read on his attitude and intentions. It's better to have an idea of what he might say, and then prepare for the worst if he doesn't follow through as promised. In addition to being a source of great stress, living with the unknown and having no official closure is an inefficient strategy for building a solid foundation for job search. In terms of how Jeffrey could address the reference issue in an interview, here are two options:

- Let me preface your request by providing a little context. My boss and I had issues around long-term strategy and direction from the start. He joined a month after I was hired. It seemed strange that he wasn't involved in recruiting me. In fact, if I was advised that he was being brought on board, I would have insisted on spending time with him. I've reached out to him to get some insight on what he'd say, but that hasn't been forthcoming. You're welcome to call him. He's in London. I'm not sure what you'll get. If you do speak to him, then it's important that you speak to someone else in a similar capacity. That's why I'm providing an additional reference of another former boss who I reported to. In my entire career, I've never had a situation like this.

- For the second strategy, Jeffrey could borrow some of the above and add the following: There's the potential that my former boss may take the separation personally and possibly sabotage the conversations. I'm concerned about that. He's a very competitive fellow. Knowing him as I do, he won't be pleased about seeing me go to a competitor. That's bound to influence what he tells you.

In both scenarios, you need to offer up additional names. The extra references you provide must have immediate credibility and the authority to speak about you as a colleague, employee, and manager. Why more? The company you're interviewing with is making a big decision. In a market like ours, they also need to know that they're making the right decision. They've identified you as a great candidate. Getting validation offers further proof that you are.

Informal Referencing

The reference checking process doesn't always play by the rules. One of the following people typically oversees the process: your future boss, the company's HR person, or the recruiting firm. Whoever it is, he or she may decide to get the "real" scoop on you and circumvent the formalities. There's not much you can do to prevent whoever it is you're interviewing with to pick up the phone and call a friend, acquaintance, or former colleague. It's an off the record "vetting" without your permission: *What's she like? How good is she? Why would she want to leave her current job?* It shouldn't surprise you. It's Wall Street. Rules are often broken. Besides, if there's no paper trail, who's to know?

When the references you've provided are ignored in favor of this "grapevine" technique, you don't have much control over the process. If you're working, you must establish boundaries from the onset of the relationship. You must insist on discretion and confidentiality for you to interview comfortably. It's not a guarantee, but at least you have it on record that unwanted disclosure could be both embarrassing and place you in an awkward situation if you're working: *I'm expecting that our conversations will be handled with absolute discretion. If my firm were to find out that we were meeting, it would have the potential to be very bad for me.*

Even if you're not employed, back-channel conversations of this kind can become awkward fast. If you have several other conversations that have moved far along, it would be inappropriate for your job search status to be surfaced prematurely. It may also be disruptive: *I have the good fortune to be moving forward in my interviews at a few firms. I'm sure you can appreciate the need to keep all of this confidential.*

Darlene: Reputation Management

Darlene and I met around the time she decided to leave her job in marketing and PR at a national association for financial professionals. It was a big decision and even bigger leap. She had been there for seven years and gained significant industry visibility. It was a good place to park while raising a young family but it was time to move on. Several options were presented to her. She chose a role as head of investor relations for a large financial organization. Jackpot! Darlene tripled her salary. Almost immediately, she found herself in a new world of senior executives as peers and her company in headline news.

Be careful what you wish for. The company reported multibillion dollar losses six months after Darlene came on board. Budgets were cut, and massive lay-offs were announced. She survived, but her world shrunk dramatically. It was like a game of musical chairs. Her colleagues were scrambling to grab any and all seats to secure their power base. Over the next couple of months, Darlene received several calls from recruiters sniffing around. Life outside seemed a lot more attractive. Although she was not the kind of person to give up without a fight, it just didn't seem worth it. Why bother when there were interesting and less-complicated opportunities available? The only colleagues who managed to thrive amid the chaos were the "lifers." They grew up in the company. They could tap longstanding relationships and institutional knowledge and call in favors to maintain and expand their worlds.

She made the move to another global financial institution in an equivalent position. Big job, more money...another home run! Within three months of joining the company, it was the target of a successful takeover attempt. Four months later, Darlene was packed up and out of her office with a substantial severance package and outplacement support. She took the summer off. Having been through two difficult corporate meltdowns back-to-back, she needed a time-out. It seemed like the right decision at the time. When she was about ready to return to job search and to work—fall 2008—that's when the financial markets imploded. The rules changed. The market literally screeched to a dead halt. Jobs disappeared, recruiters were no longer returning her calls, and when they did, they expressed great concern about the movement on her resume. Life before: Darlene walked on water. She could do no wrong. Now: She was damaged goods.

When we met, Darlene had already been in job search for several months. To her credit, she was in the loop when jobs at her level opened up. She was also called in for a respectable number of initial meetings. The problem: None of these conversations led to further interviews. Despite the stiff competition, something else was going on. There were far too many meetings that led nowhere. She needed some feedback from the market. Maybe it was a reputational matter? Or perhaps she hadn't been in real leadership roles for long enough to compete successfully with heavyweight candidates?

I encouraged Darlene to survey a few of the recruiters who recently presented potential assignments to her. The premise: to ensure that she was doing everything possible to compete and win. Here's what she discovered:

- Yes, her limited length of service as a senior manager was a challenge but not insurmountable. She couldn't use that as an excuse. A few companies still expressed interest in her.
- Agreed, the market was tough, but opportunities managed to always surface. Again, not a default to explain her lack of success in job search.
- Bingo! Several of the recruiters performed informal reference checks. They didn't rely on Darlene's names. They tapped into their own networks. Darlene's reputation was tarnished.

Darlene was fortunate that two of the recruiters she reached out to were willing to share feedback. They had independently contacted a few of her former colleagues. It was standard operating procedure. Who? Of course, those names would not be provided. The fact that they would be willing to disclose even this level of information was above and beyond what she could expect.

For someone who's used to being in control, this can be an enormously frustrating and stressful experience. Darlene was beside herself with concern. Nevertheless, she expressed her gratitude: *That's very distressful feedback to hear. I'm sure you would agree that out of context this sort of information can be extremely damaging. I would have liked the opportunity to address some of the more inflammatory comments. I care deeply about my reputation. I'm grateful that you were willing to share it with me.* These were recruiting relationships that she needed to maintain and develop further. The challenge then would be to handle future situations with this newly acquired knowledge: that informal reference checking could provide feedback that had the potential to be unwelcome and disruptive.

It was important that Darlene introduce the following theme early on in her conversations:

> As the interviewing process unfolds, you may, through informal information gathering, hear mixed feedback about my reputation: some outstanding and some not so. At my level and role in an organization, you don't always make friends. Sometimes the work can be very confrontational. Depending on whom you're talking to and whether the information is first or secondhand, some people may have an ax to grind. Alternatively, this is a highly competitive market, and some people may have ulterior motives.
>
> Should that be the case as you do your due diligence, please allow me to offer you perspective. I care deeply about my reputation, and I'd like the opportunity to address this feedback.

Although ignorance can be blissful when it comes to informal reference checking, you need to be actively involved if that information is potentially inflammatory. Like Darlene's situation, it will stop the interviewing process dead in its tracks. Although there's no guarantee that you can correct image-related issues as they arise, you have no choice but to jump in swinging if your reputation is on the line.

Recruiters

Finally, how should you handle recruiters and references? No matter how hard a recruiter pushes, please don't provide references until you've reached end-stage interviews. That's when you've been told that you're a finalist. If it's any earlier in the process, ask why! Recruiters often think they can bend the rules. In this case, it involves requesting information even if that information is not yet relevant. If any of the following bullets describe your current situation, then you have no choice but to push back—politely, of course:

- You're currently working. Any leaks that you're a candidate for another position have the potential to jeopardize where you are right now.
- Your references are busy and prominent senior executives. They've agreed to support you in your job search but only when you're a serious candidate.
- You don't want to overuse your references. If they're contacted frequently and you never seem to land, they're likely to wonder why. Are you as strong as they thought you were? That's not a question you want them to contemplate.

The only exception: You're a candidate for a position through a retainer recruiting firm. They insist that gathering the names is an integral part of the process, and that it's standard operating procedure. When that's the case, by all means, go ahead and provide them. But make sure to do so with this caveat:

I'm giving you a list of names as references as you requested. It's only to show you that my references are solid and extensive. I'm not giving you permission to contact them. Do I have your word that you will not reach out to them yet? As I'm sure you can imagine, they are busy senior executives, and I don't want to waste their time. They're committed to supporting me. However, to contact them too early in the process, if this doesn't work out, could potentially compromise my reputation with them. It also has the potential to make you look bad, too.

11

Conclusion

Financial markets are cyclical. Booms and busts to some degree are inherent to open markets. The nature of markets means they eventually stabilize. Although the financial crisis of 2008 was triggered by conditions that will most likely not be repeated—absurdly easy credit, speculative conditions in the primary home market, poor transparency for investors, and so forth—new crises are inevitable.

The markets will grow, firms will hire, and opportunities will expand. Know that. It may not feel that way to you as you read this book, but a turnaround will happen. They always do, and you should be prepared. No one can predict beyond 2011—that's the long term these days—but Wall Street will still be there, and you should be ready to pursue your dreams.

What do I know with reasonable certainty? People are greedy. That's what produced innovation and an enhanced quality of life for us, and that's why many of us have been drawn to Wall Street for our careers. Greed is good...echoes of *Wall Street* and Gordon Gecko, you say? No! It's not evil either. For the purposes of this book, and for this book only, it's just reality. Greed has produced Ponzi schemes of enormous magnitude and consequence and a willingness of traditional financial institutions to take on unprecedented risk. Greed has also been a motivating force to spur the economy, produce innovation, and identify and manage risk. Will a new economy emerge? Yes. Will there be a return to prosperity? Absolutely, emphatically yes!

If that's the case, we need to make sure you're doing everything possible to ensure that you remain whole, or as whole as you can be, in the midst of this tsunami. It means doing everything possible to ensure that you'll be taken seriously next year, the year after, and the year beyond that. So when the situation improves, which it will, you'll be ready and prepared to spring into action when others won't.

That means accepting the fact that market corrections are inevitable. It also means that short-term solutions are not necessarily damaging when it comes to our careers. The exception, of course, is engaging in criminal activity. That's something I can't help you talk your way out of...in or out of an interview (although I have worked successfully with quite a few clients whose U5's could have benefited from some "white-out" and a magician's wand).

The theme is to be working, if not in the exact role you want, then in one that's related. It's also to know that you can easily explain why you chose that direction at a time when the markets were at their very worst. Better to be in a mediocre situation than none. Better to have a good story to tell. No excuses—just the knowledge that having a job in a tough market is an accomplishment in and of itself.

Your Career Mantra

As we've considered in the preceding chapters, a Wall Street career path is no longer linear. You shouldn't expect it to be. You'll be thrown plenty of curve balls, and the goal is to catch some and avoid getting hit by the others. If you agree with me that a career is lifelong, or if your portfolio forces you to pretend to think that way, then you will also agree that we have no choice but to seek out challenges and prepare for an occasional bump along the way. When we resist or ignore change, we place ourselves in great career danger.

So, how to adapt to an unpredictable and unstable market? And as a corollary, how not to personalize the rejection that will ultimately diminish your brand value? It's all about attitude. You can choose to fight back, get angry, demand justice, or just sit it out (the equivalent of closing your eyes and hoping that the "problem" will disappear).

Alternatively, you can look at this as a game. Not to minimize the risk or the seriousness of the consequences or to suggest that the experience is unimportant, but like a game, you maximize your ability to win through skill and strategy. It helps to be lucky. It also helps to be optimistic and to believe that you deserve to win, should win, and given the right circumstances, will win. So, what then is your job search and career management mantra?

- I deserve to win...yes, I'm entitled to win.
- I'm qualified to win.
- I want to and will win.

Let's De-Construct: Entitled?

Do you believe that despite the odds and the competition, and all else being equal, that you should come out on top? That you're better than everyone else? Even if you're not, it doesn't matter. This is not about being arrogant or unaware of your real qualifications, ability, or attractiveness in the market. You must believe that it's your right to expect to achieve your goals. What's the alternative? At the end of the day, you are what you make of yourself. You're also what you tell people you are and what you decide you want to be. It's as simple as that.

Low self esteem, you say? Or alternatively, you claim to be an introvert? All of us have issues and challenges that have the potential to trip us up. For the purposes of job search, we don't ignore them. We just accept them for what they are and know that not everyone will like us. Remember the universal law of job search...it's to embrace rejection. You just can't take it personally. Even if you're the perfect candidate, given the market and the competition, you'll still get rejected. The numbers are not in your favor. Nevertheless, you must believe that it's your right to succeed *and* to fail and that you deserve it just as much as anyone else.

I'm Qualified

Success in job search requires knowing what skills and qualifications are necessary to be taken seriously for the kind of job you are seeking. It means being brutally honest regarding deficits and addressing these gaps through self-study, hands-on experience including volunteer work, continuing education, certification, or any number of other options either alone or in combination. I've worked with several clients who have pursued CFAs and CFPs in their 40's and 50's. What better message to show that your career is important to you and that you're making a commitment to the long-term?

When are you ready to go for the great job—the one of your dreams? Ask the experts, the people who are working in the kind of job you want for yourself. Look to them to point you in the right direction. But also remember that if a goal is important enough to you, then you have to trust your instincts. It's better to jump too soon and risk embarrassment than to hold back indefinitely until you feel completely ready.

At some point, for those of you who are making a career change, you do need to graduate from apprentice to candidate, and it may be sooner than you think or feel comfortable acknowledging. Practice seeing yourself as a great candidate. Not a perfect candidate...that's an ideal that no one can possibly achieve, and it's a standard that's set by companies where there are really no opportunities available. You just need a reasonable benchmark.

I Want to Win and Will Win

It's very easy to get discouraged in job search. That's because being out there means that you will face repeated rejection. In this current environment, or in any tough market for that matter, there will be many, many more qualified candidates than opportunities.

Companies have become spoiled in how they go about identifying candidates. It's the beauty pageant syndrome. If you meet the following long list of criteria *and* you happen to look great in a swimsuit, then maybe, just maybe, you'll be taken seriously. That's a company that doesn't really have a genuine job opening...just folks with too much time on their hands. They've made it almost impossible to pass the entry exam. But still, it's good interview practice for you.

It's a cruel world on Wall Street. When you take your knocks, lose a job, lose some money, or get screwed by your boss—and you will—you cannot take these events personally. Everyone fails. It's the next step that matters. The sooner you accept that dynamic, and prepare for the occasional crisis, the more quickly you will restore the status quo. Besides, Wall Street has a very short attention span and an even shorter memory. Although it is unforgiving when it needs to be, it is also a place where you have the potential to reinvent yourself. You just need to be smart about it and have a strategy.

Moving Forward

I don't know about you, but I can certainly speak for myself about the meaning of work and career. Both are central to who I am and how I define myself out in the world. I like to work and I need to work. It's lucky for me that both are aligned. You need to feel the same way, too.

401k's aside, we are in the midst of a social and professional revolution. Careers are no longer linear, and we don't just come to a hard stop at age 62 or 65. This book has been written for Wall Street professionals of any age. When you're right out of college, you need to distinguish yourself immediately and continue to do so over the course of your career.

Early on, it's all about working hard, accumulating knowledge, and establishing meaningful relationships...being willing to jump through hoops to demonstrate your commitment and showing that you are smart and hungry. Even if your employer is ungrateful! Over time, it evolves into leveraging this knowledge to convey your value whether as a revenue generator or behind the scenes as a builder or supporter of infrastructure.

But what about the Wall Street many of us are familiar with that has historically been obsessed by youth and, at its worst, views life after 40 as obsolete and treats older employees as dinosaurs? These institutions are failing, and in their place, new institutions are emerging...smaller, age friendly, and needing human capital with deep experience and the ability to hit the ground running. It's your mission to present to these companies not a cast-off from a traditional organization but instead a dynamic, energetic, focused, and valuable resource...whatever your age.

It's your career, and it's what you make of it. Yes, there are many barriers to success today, but there many opportunities, too. Don't miss out on them because you haven't taken the time to learn the new rules and incorporated this knowledge into how you manage your career.

Go forward and conquer!

INDEX

W-X-Y-Z

FT Press

FINANCIAL TIMES

In an increasingly competitive world, it is quality
of thinking that gives an edge—an idea that opens new
doors, a technique that solves a problem, or an insight
that simply helps make sense of it all.

We work with leading authors in the various arenas
of business and finance to bring cutting-edge thinking
and best-learning practices to a global market.

It is our goal to create world-class print publications
and electronic products that give readers
knowledge and understanding that can then be
applied, whether studying or at work.

To find out more about our business
products, you can visit us at www.ftpress.com.